MECHANIZED WARFARE

MECHANIZED WARFARE

Simon Dunstan

COMPENDIUM

This edition published by

COMPENDIUM

ISBN: 978-1-849120-47-0

Cataloging-in-Publication data is available from the
Library of Congress

Printed in China through Printworks Int. Ltd

Design: CompendiumDesign

Dedication: To Willy and Harry Dunstan

Acknowledgments
The author wishes to record his thanks to the following individuals and organizations for their kind assis-
tance in the preparation of this book: Nick Cornish,
Robin Cross, Yves DeBay, George and Simon Forty,
Will Fowler, MOD, NARA, Philip Royal, Steve Zaloga.
Many of the superb color photographs in this book are
courtesy of Philip Royal and copies are available via
his website—www.depthoffield.cjb.net

Much of the material from the United States came via
Mindy Day, including the atmospheric Cold War
phorographs supplied by Mark Reardon. Some of the
photographs in this book—particularly in World War II,
such as the blurred outline of the Tiger 1 at right, and
some of the early digital photography—were taken
some years ago in combat conditions: their quality
leaves something to be desired, but they have been
included within this book—alongside the perfect color
reenactment shots—to show what the real thing looks
like.

COVER: *The M4 medium tank is one of the most important AFVs in
the history of mechanized warfare and it was produced in greater
numbers than any other tank during WWII. Philip Royal*

PAGE 1: *See page 256*

PAGE 2: *The M8 was the most significant American armored car
of World War II. Over 11,000 were produced between 1943 and 1945.
The concept of mechanized warfare requires many types
of AFVs, both wheeled and tracked, to provide full flexibility on
the battlefield. Philip Royal*

*Soldiers dismount from a
Stryker infantry carrier vehicle
(ICV) to conduct a patrol in
Mosul, Iraq, on May 19, 2004.
The soldiers are assigned to
Company C, 1st Battalion, 23rd
Infantry Regiment, of the 2nd
Infantry Division's Stryker
Brigade Combat Team. This
Stryker is fitted with bar armor
as protection against RPG anti-
tank rockets.*

CONTENTS

INTRODUCTION

The tank has a long prehistory stretching from the doodles of Leonardo da Vinci to H.G. Wells's fictional "land ironclads" of the 1903 *Strand Magazine* and the Simms Motor War Car developed and then abandoned a year earlier. But the tank's transition from Renaissance flight of fancy to fully fledged armored fighting vehicle came about in World War I and was a direct response to the tactical tyranny of trench warfare.

By 1915 the Western Front had congealed into two opposing trench systems stretching from the English Channel to the Swiss frontier. Fighting was frozen into a nightmarish parody of siege warfare. Artillery ranged back and forth across the battlefield while troops in the front line exchanged fire through armored loopholes, often using periscopes to scan the enemy front. Trench warfare was dominated by machine guns and mortars, the latter lobbing bombs across no man's land, the often short distance—sometimes as little as a few yards—which separated the two lines.

As deadlock gripped the Western Front, trench engineering became ever more elaborate. The German Hindenburg Line, built in the winter of 1916–17, consisted of three lines of double trenches to a depth of two miles, the first of

RIGHT: *The three fundamental elements of any tank—firepower, mobility, and armor protection—are as ancient as warfare itself as is shown by these medieval knights parading during a tournament procession in a woodcut by H. Burgkmair—*The Triumph of Maximilian, *c. 1516–18.*

FAR RIGHT: *The appalling muddy conditions on much of the Western Front consistently compromised the mobility of men and equipment. It led to the design and development of track-laying machines for use as gun tractors and, finally, to the tank as an offensive weapon. Here, British soldiers struggle to dig out an 18pdr field gun during the Third Battle of Ypres when the rain came even in the height of the summer months.*

which was protected by six belts of barbed wire, the densest of them 100 yards thick. Dozens of communications trenches linked the lines and to the rear were sited hundreds of guns zeroed in to deliver devastating unregistered fire to no man's land with shrapnel, high-explosive, and gas shells. Further forward, machine guns with interlocking fields of fire were positioned to strafe no man's land the moment the enemy went over the top. Railways were built deep into the rear areas to speed reinforcement and resupply.

The first attempt by the British to breach the German trench line was launched at Neuve Chapelle in March 1915. An initial breakthrough was achieved before communications broke down, ammunition ran out, and the advance slithered to a halt—the pattern for bigger battles to come.

In September 1915, amid the slagheaps and shattered mining communities of Loos, the British lost another 65,000 men while supporting a French offensive in Champagne which itself led to a further 190,000 casualties. Then it was the German turn to "bleed France white" in the battle for the French fortress system at Verdun. Between February 21 and the end of June 1916 the Germans inflicted 500,000 casualties on the French defenders of Verdun at a cost of 440,000 to themselves.

The German effort at Verdun was brought to a halt by the massive British bombardment on the Somme, at the junction of the British and French lines. After the attrition at Verdun the burden of the fighting in this sector was to be shouldered by the British Third and Fourth armies in an offensive for which planning had begun in December 1915. It was here, on the Somme, that the British were to give a new weapon—the tank—its baptism of fire

In autumn 1914 a journalist, Major Ernest Swinton, had been despatched to France by Lord Kitchener as official observer with the British Expeditionary Force. Swinton witnessed the onset of trench warfare and grasped the urgent need to develop a "machine gun destroyer" to break the stalemate. He began to work up an idea based on a "self-propelled climbing block house or rifle bullet-proof cupola."

On October 19, while driving from the British General Headquarters (GHQ) in St. Omer to Calais, Swinton's thoughts turned to using the prewar American Holt Caterpillar agricultural steam tractor, which ran on "endless" tracks, as the basis for a "machine-gun destroyer" capable of overcoming barbed wire and broken ground. Early in the conflict, Holt caterpillars, which were derived from an earlier British patent, had been successfully used as artillery tractors.

Swinton approached GHQ with the idea but met with a frosty reception. His scheme eventually found a backer in Winston Churchill, First Lord of the Admiralty. In autumn 1914 armored cars operated in northern France by the Royal Naval Air Service had enjoyed some success, but subsequently had been hampered by trenches which the Germans dug across the region's road network. The Admiralty's work on this problem coincided with Swinton's proposal and led to the establishment of an Admiralty Landships Committee, a joint naval and military body, in February 1915. From Swinton's original specification came what was known, by way of disguising the true nature of the weapon under development, as the tank.

Little Willie and "Mother"

The search for a cross-country armored vehicle capable of overcoming wire, trenches, and machine guns initially developed along two lines—the "big-wheeled" vehicle and the tracked vehicle. In the 19th century, some Fowler traction engines had run on 14ft wheels, and a mock-up of a "big-wheel landship," with

RIGHT: *The Great War saw the first widespread use of vehicles powered by the internal combustion engine. It was the dawn of mechanized warfare and the first movement of British troops to the frontlines by mechanical transport occurred on October 19, 1914, by employing London omnibuses requisitioned by the army.*

FAR RIGHT: *Emblazoned in the distinctive Solomon disruptive camouflage pattern, His Majesty's Land Ship Clan Leslie of C Company, Heavy Machine Gun Corps, proceeds along Chimpanzee Valley on the Somme Front on September 15, 1916, the day that tanks first went into action. This Male Mk. I tank is fitted with an anti-grenade wire frame above the vehicle roof. At the rear are hydraulically operated steering wheels but they proved inadequate and were soon discarded.*

15ft wheels, was developed in England. In France, simultaneous experiments were conducted with a big-wheeled tractor.

This approach was soon abandoned. It was deemed that the big-wheeled vehicles would be vulnerable to artillery fire and unable to negotiate the obstacles and pitfalls of the Western Front. In Russia work had also begun on another big-wheeled machine which was tested in 1917 and proved equally unsatisfactory.

Now the endless track solution came into its own. Swinton had proposed an adapted Holt track to carry a steel box armed with cannon and machine guns across no man's land over trench lines and into the enemy artillery, overcoming machine guns and infantry in its progress, enabling the infantry following up this armored fighting vehicle (AFV) to push on to secure their objectives.

Two candidates emerged. The first was originally dubbed the "Tritton Machine," after William Tritton, the managing director of Foster and Co., the Lincoln-based manufacturer of agricultural machinery given the task of translating Swinton's idea into reality. Designed by the motor engineer and pioneer of RNAS armored cars, Walter Wilson, it was completed in mock-up at the end of August 1915, closely followed by the machine itself. It underwent trials near Lincoln, the home of its manufacturer Foster and Co., in September.

The Tritton Machine's hull was a rectangular boilerplated box surmounted by a turret and carried on "creeping grip" tracks supplied by the Bullock Tractor Company of Chicago. It was powered by a 105hp Daimler six-cylinder engine, and a pair of wheels was attached at the rear to improve balance, assist in crossing trenches, and aid steering.

The Tritton Machine was the first vehicle to be designed and completed as a landship, but from the outset it was plagued by design defects. A second prototype, known as *Little Willie*, dispensed with the turret and had redesigned tracks and track frames, but all to no avail. *Little Willie* was unable to meet the War Office's revised obstacle-crossing requirements to cross an eight-foot wide trench and climb a parapet of 4ft 6in and so was quickly

overshadowed by a rival machine, *Big Willie*, designed by Tritton, Wilson, and the naval architect Eustace Tennyson D'Eyncourt, another significant figure in the story of RNAS armored cars.

The 28-ton *Big Willie* emerged with a soon to be famous lozenge-shaped profile and redesigned tracks running round the top of the rhomboidal hull, from each side of which projected two naval long-barreled 6-pounder (6pdr) guns carried in half-turrets or sponsons and four Vickers .303in machine guns in separate ball mountings. Like its rival, *Big Willie* was powered by a six-cylinder 105hp Daimler engine and equipped with two tail wheels. There was a crew of eight, with the commander and driver seated in the front of the cab between petrol tanks, a hazardous configuration which was soon changed.

At the end of January 1916, during trials conducted on a specially built obstacle course in Hatfield Park in Hertfordshire, *Big Willie* outperformed its smaller relative, easily negotiating barbed wire entanglements, simulated trenches and a morass created by damming a stream. It also acquired the nickname *Mother* and appropriately became the progenitor of all the British heavy tanks of World War I. Swinton later wrote of the trials:

"It was a striking scene when the signal was given and a species of gigantic cubist steel slug slid out of its lair and proceeded to rear its grey bulk over the bright-yellow clay of the enemy parapet before the assemblage of Cabinet Ministers and highly placed sailors and soldiers collected under the trees."

Skepticism and success

Not everyone found *Mother* as impressive as Swinton. The Secretary of State for War, Lord

RIGHT: *Whippet light tanks of the 3rd Battalion of the Tank Corps entered action for the first time at Maillet Mailly on March 26, 1918, in support of New Zealand infantry troops. The Tank Medium Mark A or Whippet was designed as a faster and more mobile tank to exploit any breakthroughs achieved by the heavy tanks.*

Kitchener, regarded the tank as no more than "a pretty mechanical toy," although the Chief of the Imperial General Staff, Lt-Gen Sir William R. Robertson, was impressed by *Mother's* trench-crossing abilities. On February 11, three days after a special demonstration had been staged for King George V, a request for tanks had been received from the British Expeditionary Force (BEF) in France and shortly afterward an order was placed for 100 vehicles: 50 of them designated "male" and carrying the two naval 6pdrs; the remainder designated "female," in which the naval 6pdrs were replaced with four machine guns (two in each sponson).

These Mk. I tanks would form the Heavy Section of the Machine Gun Corps, commanded by Swinton, who had been given the temporary rank of colonel and the task of raising six companies, each of them fielding 25 tanks. Early recruitment was made through the pages of *Motor Cycle* magazine and initial training exercises were conducted in a secluded base in Suffolk between Elveden and Culford.

Swinton then turned to the development of a simple set of tank tactics and guidelines for co-operation with the infantry published in February 1916 as *Notes on the Employment of Tanks*, a simplified version of which emerged as 25 "Tank Tips," many still applicable on today's battlefields. The first six convey their flavor:

"Remember your orders.
Shoot quick.
Shoot low. A miss which throws dust in the enemy's eyes is better than one which whistles in his ear.
Shoot cunning.
Shoot the enemy while they are rubbing their eyes. Economize ammunition and don't kill a man three times.
Remember that trenches are curly and dugouts deep—look round corners."

LEFT: *A Female Mk. V* tank of the 4th Battalion leads several companion Mk. V tanks through the village of Meaulte soon after its capture by the 5th Royal Berkshire Regiment on August 28, 1918. The "V*" denotes that this was a lengthened version of the standard Mk. V to allow wider trench crossing capability but its greater weight and more difficult steering because of the increased length made it less popular to operate.*

Rudimentary tank training continued against the preparations for and launching of the British offensive on the Somme. The British high command confidently expected that the initial bombardment, which expended over 1.5 million shells—many of them duds—would break up the German barbed wire, bludgeon the enemy batteries into silence, and entomb the defenders in their dugouts. They were wrong on all counts.

At 07:30 on the broiling hot morning of July 1, 1916, the British bombardment moved on to the German second line. The German machine gunners emerged from their dugouts, shaken but unscathed, to pour a withering fire into the 13 British divisions advancing at walking pace across no man's land.

By nightfall the British had lost 60,000 men, 20,000 of them dead. The offensive ground on, making only minor gains. The C-in-C of the BEF, General Sir Douglas Haig, turned to the tank to break the deadlock in spite of the fact that the new weapon was untried and available only in small numbers. In mid-August the first of four companies of tanks arrived in France, the pioneers of a new form of warfare. Swinton reminded the crews that they were "going forth to battle with the express and special object of helping their unprotected comrades in the infantry."

Swinton's tank companies assembled at Yvrench, near Abbeville, under the command of Colonel John Brough. In spite of the secrecy which was supposed to cloak their deployment, they rapidly became objects of intense curiosity to officers from visiting French and British formations and, to Swinton and Brough's alarm, spent much valuable time performing stunts for the onlookers, being treated like "a new kind of toy," as the exasperated Swinton observed. At the same time, and without consulting Swinton, Haig decided to use 42 of the 49 available tanks in penny packets across the fronts of the British XIV, XV, and III Corps to deal with enemy strongpoints and provide fire support for the infantry. The remainder were to be held in reserve.

On August 13, the tanks were moved by train to their concentration area around a railhead known as "The Loop" near Bray-sur-Somme. That night they advanced to their assembly

areas. Some broke down or sank into craters, and only 36 reached their starting positions.

They went into action on the morning of September 15, with mixed results. Tank C5 (*Crème de Menthe*) took a heavily defended factory at Courcelette and several others took large numbers of surprised and demoralized German infantry prisoner. The most notable success was scored by tank D17 (*Dinnaken*) of D Company, commanded by a Lt Hastie, which rumbled down the high street in the German-held village of Flers before receiving orders to withdraw and, shortly afterward, taking a direct hit on the track. D17 lay out for some time under heavy fire before Hastie succeeded in extricating his vehicle.

Hastie was awarded a Military Cross for his bravery at Flers and D17's feats were celebrated in the British press, which proclaimed with pardonable exaggeration:

"A Tank is walking up the High Street of Flers with the British Army cheering behind."

Although many of the tanks used on September 15 had suffered mechanical failure and had exerted little influence on the battle of the Somme, which dragged on until November 18, Haig was sufficiently impressed with their overall performance to sanction an order, submitted on September 19, for another 1,000 improved versions plus 100 improved Mk. Is to maintain production while a new design was finalized. Three weeks later the Army Council rescinded Haig's order, but it was immediately reinstated by David Lloyd George, Secretary of State for War.

WORLD WAR I

The interim 100 vehicles, designated Mk. II and III and dispensing with the Mk. I's tail wheels, were delivered between January and March 1917, with the aim of using them for training purposes. The first of the Mk. IVs—again designed by Wilson and Tritton—began arriving at the end of April 1917. Superficially, they resembled the Mk. Is, and used the same engine and transmission system, but battlefield experience on the Somme had led to significant modifications.

Armor protection was extended to counter armor-piercing bullets, and the long-barreled 6pdrs—which were prone to damage if the tank ditched—were replaced by short 6pdrs mounted in sponsons which were modified to swing inward for rail transport. In both male and female versions, Lewis guns were replaced the Vickers machine guns, a retrograde step because when mounted in a tank their cooling jackets could not be protected and were vulnerable to small-arms fire. In later tanks the Lewis gun gave way to a modified Hotchkiss with a belt feed and pistol grip.

Conditions in the Mk. I had been extremely primitive. The crew, crouching in leather helmets and chain visors, were exposed to deafening noise, choking smoke and enervating heat from the frequently red-hot engine. In action the men endured an almost permanent pandemonium in which orders were issued by means of blows to attract attention followed by frantic gesticulation. The Mk. IV included better emergency escape hatches, an improved cooling and ventilation system, and upgraded vision arrangements.

Cylindrical beams, known as "torpedo spuds," were attached to each of the Mk. IV's tracks to give them better purchase on the ground and to enable the tank to recover from ditching. This arrangement was soon overtaken by a single wide beam attached to both tracks by chains. Twin rails over the top of the hull carried the beam clear of the driver's cab.

Cambrai

Some 1,015 Mark IVs were delivered, 595 of them male and 420 female. On the Western Front the hopes of breakthrough remained as distant as ever. The Allied plans for a joint offensive in spring 1917 were dislocated by the German withdrawal to the Hindenburg Line, which began on March 16. The French ignored this development and on April 16 launched an offensive on a 40-mile front east of Soissons.

In four days, the French Fifth and Sixth Armies suffered 120,00 casualties. The French Army—already undermined by the sacrifices made at Verdun—suffered a series of mutinies. Within a month 54 French divisions, half the French Army, could no longer be counted on by its high command.

The British fared no better. An offensive launched in the Ypres salient on July 31 was soon floundering in a quagmire of Flanders mud which had been created by the artillery's progressive destruction of the region's fragile drainage system. The attack ground on until the beginning of November, with progress being measured in hundreds of yards before it was halted only five miles from the original start line. Each mile had cost the British 50,000 casualties.

In the Third Battle of Ypres, three brigades of the Heavy Branch—now renamed the Tank Corps—served with the British Fifth Army, commanded by General Sir Hubert Gough, whose staff dismissed out of hand the "swamp maps" prepared by the Tank Corps to indicate which sectors of the battlefield were effectively "untankable." Many tanks lurched into action with streams of foul slime oozing into their vehicles through every hole in the armor like a ghastly giant toothpaste tube in reverse. The ground surrounding an enemy strongpoint known as Clapham Junction was littered with the hulks of 18 tanks, destroyed by German artillery. Standing logic on its head, some senior officers blamed the tanks for the British failure at Third Ypres, but it was from the Tank Corps that there came an initiative to break the deadlock on the Western Front.

The Tank Corps now numbered some 20,000 men, the overwhelming majority drawn from civilian life, including its entire administrative and

A preserved Male Mk. V tank of the Tank Museum at Bovington in Dorset, England provides the backdrop to a color party of the Royal Tank Regiment of today. The red and white stripes on the roof and track horns were a standard recognition device for Allied troops and aircraft. The H41 on the sides denotes that this Mk. V belonged to 8th or H Battalion of the Tank Corps in 1918.

engineering staff. It was now commanded by Lt-Col H.J. Elles, himself an engineer and formerly a staff officer at GHQ. The blinkered views of GHQ on the new form of armored warfare prompted Elles to remark that "fighting the Germans is a joke compared with fighting the British."

Elles's chief general staff officer, appointed in December 1916, was Major J.F.C. Fuller of the Oxford and Buckinghamshire Light Infantry. Fuller was curious cog in the British military machine: a passionate admirer of Napoleon Bonaparte, from whom he derived his nickname of "Boney," Fuller was a man of probing intellect and wide-ranging interests, stretching from military history to Eastern religion and the occult. A thinker and intellectual controversialist rather than a man of action, Fuller was to exercize a decisive influence on the development of the armored idea. Fuller also designed the red, brown, and green Tank Corps colors, which he said symbolized blood, mud, and the green fields beyond.

At the end of 1916, Fuller had issued his first *Instructions on Training*—GHQ had thoughtfully mislaid Swinton's earlier *Notes on the Employment of Tanks*—in which he argued that the tank was a mobile fortress which could be best used in conjunction with infantry as a weapon of surprise. Fuller urged that the artillery bombardment which preceded any tank attack should be limited to 48 hours—a position calculated to irritate GHQ, which retaliated by withdrawing the paper from circulation. Fuller also argued that tanks should not be used in driblets but en masse, "in echelon and with strong reserves."

In spite of GHQ's misgivings, Haig was desperate for a success in the field to offset the disasters of 1917. It was in this mood that the British C-in-C turned to the suggestion by Elles that the Tank Corps could be used to breach the Hindenburg Line by surprise on the firm, unbroken chalk ground around the city of Cambrai, an important communications hub in a "quiet" sector in the center of the German line.

The plan was devised in detail by Fuller. He later claimed that his inspiration had been the Persian King Cyrus in 500 BC, and it took the form

LEFT: *Austin armored cars of the British Army prepare to advance near Chateau la Fôret on July 27, 1918. There was little opportunity for the use of armored cars during the years of trench warfare but once the major British offensive of August 1918 succeeded, armored cars came into their own in the pursuit of the broken German army.*

BELOW LEFT: *A Renault FT17 tank moves up to the front as German prisoners carry casualties to the rear on the first day of the American offensive at St. Mihiel. With no immediate manufacturing capacity for tanks, the American army used both French and British models.*

BELOW: *A Female Mk. V* Tank of the 4th Battalion advances through a shattered French village during the decisive Battle of Amiens on August 22, 1918. Between its rear track horns this tank carries a spare sprocket drive wheel. All the hatches are open for maximum ventilation as the interior of all tanks of the period were contaminated with carbon monoxide poisoning from the exposed engine.*

ABOVE LEFT: *A British Male Mk. V Tank takes part in a combined arms training exercise with the 107th Infantry Regiment of the 27th Infantry Division, U.S. Army, behind the Somme battlefront on September 15, 1918, two years to the day after tanks first went into action on the Western Front.*

LEFT: *A German* Flammenwerfer *(flamethrower) crew engages a Female Mk. IV tank during a demonstration on the Somme front. The Germans initially failed to grasp the military significance of the tank, and their designs and manufacturing capacity never matched those of the Allies during the war. Many measures were taken to counter the tanks, but the use of flamethrowers at such close ranges smacks of desperation and this is probably a propaganda photograph for home consumption.*

ABOVE: *A British Female Mark V Tank supports the successful American-Australian attack on the Hindenburg Line near le Catelet in France shortly before the armistice. A female tank was armed solely with machine guns to engage enemy infantry while a male tank mounted 6pdr guns as well as machine guns to engage all manner of battlefield targets.*

RIGHT: *U.S. Renault FT17 of C Company, 327th Tank Battalion, 1st Tank Brigade negotiates a trench on the opening day of the St. Mihiel Offensive near Seicheprey in France. The playing card insignia on the turret denotes the tank company within the battalion.*

of what he described as "a concentrated tank raid." Fuller envisaged an attack by nearly 500 tanks and infantry to a depth of four miles unannounced by the customary lengthy bombardment. The assault forces would concentrate by night in wooded terrain while by day British fighters drove German reconnaissance aircraft from the sky. The artillery was to withhold its contribution until the first wave of tanks began to move forward. Their task was to flatten the wire, bridge the 12ft-wide antitank ditches with huge bundles of brushwood (fascines) carried atop their hulls and subdue the German machine guns and artillery until the arrival of the second wave of tanks and supporting infantry. Smoke fired by the artillery would neutralize German observation posts while aircraft would attack enemy communication centers, trenches, and gunpits. As each of the three German defense lines was overcome, the infantry would follow up, the preliminary to the arrival of the third wave of tanks which would move on to overrun the rearward German lines and forward artillery positions. This was to be followed by the release of a mass of cavalry into open country, the capture of Cambrai and the expulsion of German forces from northern France. It was an operation planned by Fuller to unfold like clockwork.

The Mk. IVs could run for only some 20 miles before their tracks gave out, and they were brought up to the front at night by rail with minimum noise. Flights of low-flying aircraft helped to cover the noise of the last leg of their journey from the rail flats to the woods. The interrogation of British prisoners gave the Germans a hint that something was afoot, but they anticipated nothing more than a local attack on a narrow sector near Flesquieres.

The British bombardment opened at 06:20 on November 20. The Germans were persuaded to take to their dugouts in the expectation that the bombardment would last for days, enabling the British to achieve tactical surprise and overrun successive lines of defense. However, Fuller's finely balanced clockwork began to break down when the tanks on the right flank reached the vital Escaut Canal fully one hour ahead of the infantry. They were halted after a bridge collapsed under the weight of one of their vehicles.

A duel developed between the tanks and German artillery in which the British infantry and cavalry became mere bystanders.

The advance on the left flank was also compromized by the same failure to coordinate tanks, artillery, infantry, and cavalry, a factor exacerbated by the lack of portable radio sets. Some tanks had been equipped for the first time with radio equipment but were used as report centers and had no influence on the battle. Hours were lost as tanks were pulled back to replenish and troops kicked their heels waiting for orders by telephone to move against positions not laid down in the initial planning.

Nevertheless, on November 20, 1917, the British had broken through the Hindenburg Line on a frontage of seven miles, and taken over 10,000 prisoners, 123 guns, 179 mortars, and 281 machine guns for the loss of 4,000 infantry and 65 tanks. By the following day, however, the Germans had rushed up reinforcements, checked the tanks, and regained much of the ground the British had taken on the first day of the battle. Fuller remained buoyant, pointing out that for a small cost the tanks had made a penetration comparable to that which had taken three months and a massive toll in dead during the Third Battle of Ypres. The English church bells, which had been rung in premature celebration on November 21, had nevertheless recognized the tanks at Cambrai as harbingers of a new era in warfare.

The French, Germans, and Americans

The French had also been experimenting with armored tracked vehicles. In 1915 the Schneider company of Le Creusot obtained two Holt tractors, enabling the designer Eugene Brillie to develop a "*Char d'assaut*" (CA), the first examples of which were delivered in September 1916, at about the time that the British tanks went into action on the Somme.

The Schneider tank was, in essence, a 15-ton armored box with a pointed nose mounted on a lengthened Holt Caterpillar chassis and powered by a four-cylinder 70hp engine giving it a maximum speed of just under 5mph and a range of about 30 miles. A short 75mm gun was fitted in a sponson on the right-hand side of the hull, with

an 8mm Hotchkiss machine gun fitted further back on the same side and another Hotchkiss on the other side. There was a crew of six, and the tank was driven by its commander.

The Schneider tanks received their baptism of fire on April 16, 1917, at Berry au Bac on the River Aisne. The French C-in-C on the Western Front, General Robert Nivelle, committed 132 Schneiders, in two groups, to an attack which was intended to advance across the flat ground between the Aisne at Neufchatel and Soissons. The attack was not a success, suffering heavy losses—the larger group under Commandant Louis-Marie-Ildefonse Bossut lost 44 of its 81 vehicles—and exposing many of the Schneider tank's weaknesses: its poorly protected fuel tanks, located high on each side, quickly caught fire ("brewed up" in British tankers' parlance) when the Schneider was penetrated by machine gun bullets; and the 75mm gun had a very limited traverse.

OPPOSITE, LEFT: *The most numerous French tank was the Renault FT17. It had a crew of two with a driver in the hull and a commander cum gunner in the revolving turret. It came in two versions; the Char-Mitrailleuse armed with a single 8mm machine gun and the Char-Canon armed with a 37mm Puteaux gun as shown here.*

OPPOSITE, ABOVE RIGHT: *Because of their failure to produce tanks in any quantity, the Germans were obliged to use captured French and British ones. They were often rearmed with German weapons and adorned with large German crosses before being employed against their former owners.*

OPPOSITE, BELOW RIGHT: *Construction of the first French tanks began in early 1916 at two companies, Schneider and St Chamond. The Schneider CA 1 (Char d'assaut) weighed 13.5 tons and was armed with a 75mm gun and two 8mm machine guns. The Schneider first saw action on April 14, 1917 at the battle of Berry au Bac.*

INSET: *Due to its low weight of 6.5 tons, the Renault FT17 was highly mobile compared to the majority of Great War tanks. The FT17 first saw action on May 31, 1918, during the battle for the forest of Retz.*

LEFT: *Renault FT17 light tanks were also used by the American Expeditionary Force. These two FT17s show the two types of turrets with the first one being cast and the second composed of riveted angled armor plates.*

Nevertheless, the engagement at Berry au Bac produced France's first tank hero in Commandant Bossut, who had spent most of the initial advance on foot, urging on the tanks under his command. After nearly five hours Bossut remounted his tank, only for it to be immediately hit by plunging shell fire which killed the crew and their commander. Bossut had not managed to fire a single shot at the enemy.

In February 1916 the French had placed an order for a second heavy tank with the firm of Forges et Acieries de la Marine et d'Homecourt, at Saint Chamond near Lyon. Because of departmental and industrial rivalries—an order for 400 tanks had been placed without the full knowledge of the French Army's high command—the project was compromized from the outset, and there was no cooperation between Schneider and its new rivals.

A specially strengthened Holt chassis formed the basis of the design and a prototype was completed for testing in September 1916. The pronounced overhang of the hull at front and rear resulted in poor handling and cross-country performance, and when the Saint-Chamond went into action for the first time on May 5, 1917, more faults revealed themselves. Among them were the extreme difficulty of exiting the vehicle in an emergency, poor vision, and the recoil cylinder on the 75mm gun which was vulnerable to enemy fire. An electric transmission had eliminated the gear-changing difficulties, which had dogged the early tanks and made gear-changing and steering immensely difficult, but was fragile and unreliable in combat.

INSET, ABOVE AND BELOW: *Experiences on the Western Front showed the desirability of four-wheel drive trucks to support frontline units. These trucks are part of the 305th Ammunition Train during a review of the 80th Division at Camp Lee, Virginia, in June 1918.*

RIGHT: *The tank would become the lynchpin of mechanized warfare—but during World War I muddy trench lines all too often led to bogging down.*

Numerous design changes were introduced during the production run and also applied retrospectively: the gun was replaced and one of the two cupolas on the roof was removed to give the crew more headroom; the narrow tracks were widened and given a chevron pattern for greater traction; and a recommendation was made—but not fully carried out—to strengthen the tank's sides with armor plating. The final weight of Saint-Chamond was 24 tons. Neither the Saint-Chamond nor the Schneider tank were successful designs, and when contemplating the offensive planned for 1919, but never undertaken, the French accepted the British offer of heavy tanks.

In the development of tanks the Germans lagged behind the British and the French, but their high command was forced to respond to the British tank actions of September 1916, in spite of the fact that their tactical impact had been small. A committee of experts drawn from heavy engineering and automotive companies considered designs based on a Holt tractor from Austria. Designed by Josef Vollmer, a wooden mock-up emerged in the spring of 1917 and, as the A7V Sturmpanzerwagen, went into production.

The A7V was in essence a massively armored mobile gun platform designed to perform in an infantry-support role. It weighed 33 tons combat-loaded and was crewed by 18 men. Its frontal armor was 30mm thick and the remainder varied between 15mm and 20mm. The A7V's main armament was a front-firing 5.7cm Russian Sokol, a supply of which had been captured on the Eastern Front, while six water-cooled Maxim '08 machine guns fired from each side and the rear.

The A7V made its combat debut at St. Quentin on March 21, 1918, at the start of the so-called Ludendorff offensive, Germany's attempt to launch a knock-out blow on the Western Front before the build-up of American troops closed off the possibility of victory. Three days later there was a significant encounter, the first tank-versus-tank action in history and the first time the Germans used tanks in any number.

On April 24 the Germans were threatening the rail center of Amiens at the junction of the British and French lines. Capture of the high ground around the village of Villers Bretonneux, some seven miles west of Amiens, would

enable German artillery to fire directly on the city. The French rushed up troops to plug the gap while the British sent in a company of Mk. IV tanks with the aim of laying a trap for the Germans, waiting in ambush positions to launch what was dubbed a "savage rabbit" strike on the German flanks.

Just after 09:30, male tank No. 40466, commanded by Lt Frank Mitchell and accompanied by two female tanks, ran into four A7Vs and German infantry advancing through fog on the village of Cachy. Almost immediately Mitchell's tank was hit by a hail of armor-piercing bullets. He ordered the crew to lie on the floor of their tank and the driver to plunge straight ahead, enabling him to draw clear of immediate danger. Mitchell was now facing three A7Vs as the fourth, *Elfried*, had blundered into a quarry and played no further part in the action.

While the British female tanks pulled back, battle was joined between 40466 and A7V *Nixe*, commanded by Lt Wilhelm Biltz. Mitchell's left-hand gunner scored three direct hits on *Nixe*, which came to halt with its engine still running and disgorged its surviving crew, who were afraid that a box of armed hand grenades in the front compartment was about to explode. In the firefight, *Nixe* had come off second best: the front gunner had been killed and two crewmen mortally wounded, with three more suffering minor injuries. Biltz and his surviving crew eventually rejoined their A7V and pulled back some two kilometers before her engine gave up the ghost.

This was not the end of the armored engagement at Villers Bretonneux. Mitchell drove off two more A7Vs before turning his attention to the German infantry, which at about 11:00 came under attack from the northern edge of Cachy by seven British Medium A Whippet tanks. The Whippets took a heavy toll of the infantry but were unaware of the remaining presence of two A7Vs (*Siegfried* and *Schnuck*) which had a hand in knocking out two of the Whippets, forcing the remainder to pull back. Two more broke down and were abandoned during the withdrawal.

It was also the end of Mitchell's battle. He had already been mistakenly attacked by a British aircraft, before coming under fire from another

German tank and an infantry mortar, the latter shattering one of his tracks. At 12:45 Mitchell and his crew regained the safety of the British trenches. Mitchell was subsequently awarded the Military Cross for his gallantry at Villers Bretonneux.

The engagement at Villers Bretonneux had been significant not only for Mitchell's tank-ver-sus-tank encounter but also for the British employment of the of the Whippet medium tank, which along with the Renault FT17 light tank, made its combat debut in 1918 and pointed the way to the future of tank development.

The Whippet had been designed by William Foster and Co. to exploit a breakthrough of the front-line enemy defenses by British heavy tanks, the Mk. IV and its successor the Mk. V. Its speed would enable the Whippet to replace the cavalry, whose limitations in this role had been exposed at Cambrai. The Whippet could move faster, further, and with greater chance of sur-vival against fire than cavalry.

The Whippet began arriving in quantity on the Western Front in March 1918. Weighing 14 tons, it had a crew of three, four machine guns, and was thinly armored. It had excellent cross-country performance with a maximum speed hovering just over 8mph. An overhaul of the suspension in the Whippet B and the substitution of a 360hp Rolls Royce aero engine, conferred a top speed of 30mph.

By August 1918 the French were taking delivery of a battalion (75) of Renault FT17 light tanks a week. Their design had been closely supervized by Louis Renault, who drove the prototype himself at its trials in February 1917. The FT17 included for the first time many of the features which would become standard in tanks after World War I, and its layout remains familiar today. It was the first mass-production tank, and some 3,500 were built in France, 514 of them going to the American Expeditionary Force (for their heavy tanks the Americans relied on the British).

The simplest version of the FT17 was armed with a Hotchkiss air-cooled 8mm machine gun but later versions, including that adopted by the Americans, mounted a 37mm Puteaux cannon firing armor-piercing (AP) or high-explosive (HE)

shells. Thinly armored, the FT17 weighed 6.9 tons with a top speed of 4.7mph and a range of 22 miles. Crewed by two men, the FT17 was the first tank to be fitted with a fully traversing turret and made its combat debut on May 31, 1918. It has been described as little more than a slow armored machine gun carrier of dubious cross-country performance but it proved effective when used en masse in 1918 and presented a small target to enemy gunners. Some later versions were adapted to operate as self-propelled 75mm guns on a Renault chassis. The FT17 was to remain in service until World War II and was adopted by the armed forces of many countries in a number of different configurations.

Lessons of World War I

By spring 1918, there were five distinct types of armored fighting vehicle: the rhomboidal heavy tank, significantly improved since its introduction in 1916 and culminating in the Mark VIII Liberty tank of 1918, with more powerful engine and capable of being driven by one man; the medium tank; the light tank; the armored assault gun; and the armored car.

In 1918 the single most significant impact of the tank was to render obsolete the trench systems which had dominated the Western Front from 1915. The correct use of tanks, in numbers, on appropriate terrain, and after a short preliminary bombardment, restored the element of surprise to the attack (and also on occasion to the defense) by the employment of three elements—firepower, protection, and mobility—to which no counter had yet been devised on the Western Front. These are the basics of modern warfare, long predating World War I, but frustrated for three years by trench warfare, a combination of firepower and immo-bility. The effective employment of AFVs overrode the need to construct complex trench barriers which now could be breached even at their points of greatest strength.

In 1918, both sides were forced into an over-haul of both their offensive and defensive tactics to accommodate the technical sea change introduced by the tank. By delivering successive armored counterblows with tanks operating in dense formations, supported by artillery and

infantry, the Allies broke the five successive German offensives of 1918. The price was high on both sides, and by mid-July about a million men had died in the fighting. The tide was then turned at Amiens early in August, when some 600 Allied tanks ripped a 20-mile hole in the German line, held more lightly than it had been at Cambrai. Light tanks, armored cars, cavalry, and infantry poured through the gap, advancing six miles in a matter of hours.

The first day of the Battle of Amiens, August 8, 1918, was the "black day of the German army" and the blow which broke the German will to continue. The success of the Allied mechanized forces was just one, albeit vital, element of the relentless and overwhelming material superiority which the Allies were now able to bring to bear on the enemy. In the closing phase of the war the Allies had demonstrated the crucial importance of robust mechanized equipment, a far cry from the mud-clogged heroics of the Tank Corps on the Somme in 1916.

It was also a lesson applied in other theaters of war. In the Middle East, British tanks outstripped cavalry in pursuit of the routed Turkish armies—a desert war which anticipated the five-week, 300-mile pursuit form Megiddo to Aleppo in October 1918, when armored cars and lorries—supported by aircraft—proved more effective than the British cavalry.

LEFT AND OPPOSITE: *The only German tank to be produced in any numbers was the A7V Sturmpanzerwagen. It derived its designation from the grandiosely named committee that designed it—Allgemeine-Kriegs-Department 7, Abteilung Verkehrswesen or General War Department 7 Traffic Section. As with many projects designed by committees, it was not an effective fighting vehicle. It was armed with a 57mm gun at the front and six additional machine guns requiring a crew of 18. Only 20 examples were built during the war and it entered service in September 1917; a whole year after the first British tanks. In the first ever tank-versus-tank action at Villers Bretonneux on April 24, 1918, a section of three British tanks with one male and two females encountered three A7Vs. The two females withdrew in the face of the A7Vs' heavier firepower leaving Lt Frank Mitchell to engage A7V No. 561 named Nixe. The A7V was hit three times by 6pdr rounds causing the crew to bail out but Nixe was later recovered. With a spring-suspension system whereas British tanks had none, the A7V gave a more comfortable ride but its cross-country mobility was inferior because of its track configuration. The last concerted attack by A7Vs occurred on August 31, 1918, near Frémicourt against New Zealand troops. Two were trapped in a village when their heavy vibration caused a house to collapse in their path. The other three continued the attack but two turned around to find their infantry support and were mistakenly disabled by German artillery guns.*

THE INTERWAR YEARS

Closely involved in the planning of the armored attack at Amiens had been the now Colonel J.F.C. Fuller, who returned to England at the end of July 1918 to establish the Tank Corps on a permanent basis at the War Office.

As the war drew to a close, Fuller threw himself into another ambitious plan, which he dubbed "Project 1919." This was a massive armored drive aimed at bringing an end to the war in a single devastating stroke. Several thousand of the planned—but never built—Medium D tanks, supported by aircraft and heavy tanks, were to slice through the enemy's line on a narrow front, paralyzing his command and control systems and bringing about a strategic paralysis.

Germany's collapse in the autumn of 1918 ensured that Fuller's Project 1919 remained a pipe dream, but many later saw its as the harbinger of the *Blitzkrieg* (lightning war) tactics developed by the German Army in the 1930s. Fuller was to remain a thorn in the side of a post-1918 War Office which he dismissed as the preserve of a superannuated elite still infatuated with the horse.

Nevertheless, after the war to end all wars it was the British—alone among the world's armies—who in the early 1920s created an independent armored force, the Royal Tank Corps, to

RIGHT: *A Peerless 1919 armored car of C Troop, Westminster Dragoons, comes to grief in a ditch during internal security duties in Ireland in the 1920s. Originally designed and built by Austin during the Great War, the armored body was transferred to a more powerful American Peerless chassis to give a more robust and reliable vehicle that continued as a training vehicle up to 1939. The vehicle features twin machine gun turrets behind the driver's compartment. The insignia on the front is that of the Houses of Parliament which was adopted by the Westminster Dragoons who hailed themselves as The London Armoured Car Company.*

BELOW AND RIGHT: The crews of 2 Section, 6th Armoured Car Company, line up for inspection in front of their Crossley armored cars at a barracks in Delhi, India, during the late 1930s. The Crossley was a standard 4x2 truck chassis fitted with an Indian-pattern armored body. These armored cars served in India from 1923 to 1939 but were unpopular with their crews as the "semi-solid" tires gave an uncomfortable ride. The vehicle was underpowered with its armored body, while the brakes were totally inadequate for the extra weight and there were none on the front wheels at all. This gave rise to some hair-raising driving experiences on the precipitous and winding roads of the mountainous Northwest Frontier of India and Afghanistan. The turret features four mounting points for machine guns and it was customary to carry two with one to the front and on to the rear at opposite corners.

investigate the theories of mechanized warfare of which Fuller had been the driving intellectual force. Against Fuller's advice, however, the Corps' senior ranks were filled with otherwise redundant officers whose views were inimical to his own. Nevertheless, the Royal Tank Corps Centre at Bovington, in Dorset, was to become a forcing bed for experimentation in the hands of its first Chief Instructor, Colonel George Lindsay, who had commanded an armored car company in Iraq.

It was not until the late 1920s that Fuller's ideas of long-range penetration could move from theory to practical experimentation with the arrival in numbers of medium tanks with cross-country speeds approaching 20mph, reliable suspension and tracks and an operational radius of 150 or more miles. The vehicle that made this possible was the 12-ton Vickers Medium Tank, with 8mm armor, a rotating turret housing a coaxially mounted 3pdr 47mm cannon and machine gun. It was crewed by a commander, gunner, and radio operator/loader. In trials with the Experimental Mechanised Force, medium and light armor, vehicle-borne infantry, artillery engineers, and aircraft were used together, but in 1928 the forces of military conservatism carried the day and the force was disbanded.

Fuller had originally been offered the command of the Experimental Mechanised Force but had turned it down as it would have also entailed commanding an infantry brigade. This effectively ended his direct influence on the armored idea within the British Army but only spurred his efforts as a popular polemicist for his theories. In this he was assisted by a new ally, Captain Basil Liddell Hart, another veteran of World War I who became an influential military historian, journal-

FAR RIGHT: *The recovery of tanks on the battlefield is a vital task to maintain the momentum of an advance and to deny their use to the enemy. Similarly tanks with mechanical problems such as this Vickers Light Tank must be rapidly recovered to prevent them from falling into enemy hands.*

RIGHT: *The Vickers Medium Tank Mk. I entered service in 1924 and was the first British tank with a fully revolving turret. It was armed with a 3pdr quick-firing (QF) gun and six machine guns served by a five-man crew.*

ist, and spokesman for the mechanizing wing of the Royal Tanks Corps.

The main British tank strength into the mid-1930s remained the Vickers Medium Mk. III, with the scouting role being undertaken by light tanks, some of which also served on colonial policing duties. However, it was clear by now that the medium and light tanks would be highly vulnerable on a modern battlefield, particularly in tank-versus-tank confrontations.

The result was a 1934 General Staff specification for a medium tank to succeed the Vickers while fulfilling a changed role. The project was dogged by the financial stringencies imposed by the economic slump of the period and by considerable confusion on the part of the General Staff as to its precise role in any future war.

The General Staff's cautious deliberations threw up a family of tanks which harked back to the experience of World War I: the cruiser tank was intended to fulfill the role of cavalry but with the additional ability to engage other tanks; in another nod to the battlefields of 1917–18, slow-moving infantry tanks were to move forward with the attacking infantry, using their main armament of machine guns to silence enemy machine gun nests; finally, light tanks were to be used in a reconnaissance role.

First in this tank hierarchy was A9 Cruiser Mk. I, the first British tank equipped with a power-operated turret and an auxiliary engine. However, these innovations were offset by a number of design defects inherent in the tank's compromised origins. In order to accommodate a commercial AEC bus engine, the A9's weight was reduced to at the expense of armor protection. The vertical armor itself offered numerous angles and corners in which AP shot could lodge rather than glance off.

The fighting and driving compartments were combined into one, and a fan driven by the auxiliary motor was needed to clear the fumes from the cruiser's turret-mounted 2pdr gun and .303in machine gun and the two .303s mounted in subsidiary turrets in the hull. Conditions for the six-man crew (commander, gunner, driver, and two hull machine gunners) were cramped and reminiscent of a World War I Mk. IV. A few A9s were modified for a close-support role, with their

2pdrs being replaced by a short-barreled 3.7in howitzer.

From 1938 the A9 served with British 1st Armoured Division. It was followed into service with 1st Armoured by the A13 Mk. II, better known as the Cruiser Mk. IV, which was derived from a high-speed American Christie tank purchased in 1936. The Christie had a reputation for throwing its crew around when traveling at speed cross-country, and the Mk. IV incorporated a redesigned hull and turret, the latter featuring undercut sides and sloped upper plates. Powered by a reliable American Liberty aero-engine of World War I vintage, the Mk. IV entered production in 1938, setting the standard for later cruiser tanks of World War II and entering service with 1st and 7th Armoured divisions in 1939–40.

The British Army's first infantry tank of the interwar years was the A11 Matilda, which entered service in 1938. Matildas were produced at a unit cost of £6,000 per tank, and this was reflected in its many shortcomings. It had an overworked two-man crew and was armed with one .3in or .5in Vickers machine gun. It was clearly not cost-effective to spend money on the volume production of a tank armed only with a machine gun and boasting a road speed of 8mph, barely faster than that of a running man. The fact that the A11's 60mm frontal armor was virtually impervious to any antitank weapon of the time was not sufficient to offset the disadvantaged inherent in the idea of the infantry tank.

The A11 was followed into service by the A12 Matilda II, which underwent trials in 1938, the year in which Britain begin to accelerate its rearmament program. During its development the War Office sensibly decided that the Matilda should be uparmored, to deal with antitank weapons, and upgunned to deal with enemy tanks and gun positions. The A12 Matilda which went into production in 1939–40 featured a cramped, heavy, cast turret rotated by hydraulic power, housing three of its four crew and fitted, in the Mk. I version, with a 2pdr gun and a Vickers .303in machine gun. Both the A11 and the A12 were to see action in 1940 in the Battle of France.

In World War I, France had been a volume producer of tanks, particularly the two-man Renault

The Vickers Medium Tank was the mainstay of The Royal Tank Corps until the late 1930s when rearmament began in earnest. Under the guidance of such tank experts as G. le Q. Martel and J.F.C. Fuller, a revolutionary armored doctrine was devised during the late 1920s. It was not adopted by the British Army and emerged as the basis for Blitzkrieg in Germany.

FT17, of which over 4,000 had rolled off the production lines. It also had its prophet of armored warfare to match the British Fuller—Colonel (later General) Estienne. However, after 1918 Estienne was sidelined as the French chose to ignore all the significant lessons of the 1914–18 war. In part this was because the postwar French Army became a prisoner of the great mass of aging machinery it inherited from the battles of 1918. These battles loomed large in the French military mind. In 1921 Marshal Pétain, commander-in-chief of the French Army and the hero of Verdun, stated in his *Instructions*: "Tanks assist the advance of the infantry, by breaking static obstacles and active resistance put up by the enemy." In the mind of Pétain and the French General Staff, the pace of the modern battlefield was still regulated by the speed of the infantryman rather than the armored spearheads, supported by aircraft and motorized infantry formations, which were envisaged by Fuller and Liddell Hart in the interwar years.

In the interwar years, the French military mindset was almost exclusively defensive. To defend the sacred soil of France it resorted to rationalizing, in concrete and steel, the trench systems of 1917–18. Constructed between 1929 and 1940, the Maginot Line provided a fixed defensive line on the Franco-German border behind which maneuver armies could form and deploy. As General Maurin, France's Minister of War, declared in 1935:

"How can we still believe in the offensive when we have spent thousands of millions to establish a fortified barrier? Would we be mad enough to advance beyond this barrier upon goodness knows what adventure?"

Ironically, in the interwar years the French produced excellent light, medium, and heavy tanks, some of them markedly superior to others in service with other armies. The French Army's standard medium tank was designed and built by SOMUA, the Société d'Outillage Mécanique et d'Usinage d'Artillerie. It was designated the Char S-35, the "S" standing for SOMUA and the "35" for the year it was introduced to service. By 1940

there were some 500 S-35s with the French Army.

The three-man S-35 was powered by a 190hp engine and had a 47mm main armament with a 7.5mm Model 31 coaxial machine gun. Equipping France's Divisions Légères Mécaniques It was mobile, with a maximum road speed of 23mph and a range 160 miles. Its principal weakness, echoed throughout French tank design, was that the commander was also the gunner and loader. Another weakness lay in the hull, which was cast in three sections bolted together, making the tank highly vulnerable if there were a direct hit at or around the joints. The final version of S-35, the S-40, which arrived in 1940, was driven by a powerful 220hp engine.

The principal weapon of France's Divisions Cuirasses in 1940 was the 32-ton Char B1-bis heavy tank, of which some 365 were built. They were heavily armored and capable of withstanding the fire of any antitank gun with the exception of the German 88mm. As with the S-35, the hull was of cast sections bolted together, and the Char B1 was also fitted with an identical APX turret to that mounted on the S-35 and carrying a 37mm gun and 37mm machine gun. The main 75mm SA35 short-barreled gun mounted in the glacis was to the right and below the driver, who also fired it, pointing the entire tank at the target. Below the 75mm gun was a 7.5mm machine gun. There was an overworked crew of four, of whom the commander in particular was under intense pressure, loading and firing the turret gun in addition to his other duties.

In the Soviet Union, the Red Army's interest in armored warfare was initially stimulated by the capture in 1919, during the War of Intervention, of two Renault FT light tanks. In 1920 the Russians produced a modified version, the KS, prompting the design and development of a range of AFVs. Between the late 1920s and 1937 some 21,000 had been built, comprising three standard classes: light, medium, and heavy

The Soviet Union also produced its own advocate of armored warfare, Marshal Mikhail N. Tukhachevsky, a former Tsarist officer and the Red Army's chief of staff in the mid-1930s. Tukhachevsky had been influenced by the writ-

ings of Fuller and Liddell Hart and contact in the 1920s with German officers training in clandestine conditions in the Soviet Union in defiance of the 1919 Treaty of Versailles.

Tukhachevsky developed his own strategic theory of "deep operations," spearheaded by armor and supported by aircraft. He began to form Red Army mechanized corps, but the Soviet Union lacked the industrial infrastructure to realize his ideas. Nor was the political climate propitious, and in 1937 Tukhachevsky became the most notable victim of Stalin's purges of the Red Army, and was summarily court-martialed and shot. Tukhachevsky's ideas were discredited and the corps he had formed were broken up.

Nevertheless, in the 1930s the groundwork was laid for the Soviet Union's great tank victories in the latter part of World War II. The first steps had been taken early in the decade with the *Bystrochodny* (fast) tank series. The BT cruiser tanks exploited the ingenious M1931 suspension system developed in the United States by the engineer Walter Christie, which conferred exceptionally high cross-country speed. The system consisted of large solid-rubber-tired roadwheels independently attached to pivoting lever arms in the side of the hull, cushioned by heavy coil springs, the later located between the inner and outer walls of the hull.

The Soviet Union purchased two M1931 vehicles, shipped them back to the Kharkov Locomotive Works and used them as the basis for the BT series, which also incorporated a steering wheel in conjunction with a clutch-and-brake system for directional control. The three-man BT-7 of 1936 was powered by a 350hp aero-engine (later models were fitted with the V2 12-cylinder 500hp engine) and carried a

FAR LEFT: *The Valentine was the third in the series of British infantry tanks. Built by Vickers, the original models—such as* Cameronian *of the 17th/21th Lancers—were armed with a 2pdr gun while later versions mounted a 6pdr and finally a 75mm gun.*

LEFT: *The A22 Infantry Tank Mk. IV Churchill was designed to meet the conditions similar to the Great War as a "shelled area tank." Rushed into production, the Churchill suffered from many teething problems but later emerged as an effective tank that was adapted to numerous different roles.*

76.2mm main armament and 7.62mm machine gun. On tracks they could reach 37mph and on wheels 69mph.

In theory the BT tank was designed to operate in large, independent, long-range, armored, and mechanized formations, using their speed to penetrate and shoot up the enemy rear areas, cutting communications and paralyzing command and control. From 1935, these groups were supplied with artillery fire support in the form of the BT-5A carrying a short-barreled 76.2mm howitzer. However, the upheavals which overtook the Red Army's armored formations after the purges of the late 1930s did little to turn theory into practice on the battlefield.

Nevertheless, before the German invasion of the Soviet Union in 1941, BT tanks saw action in the Spanish Civil War—fighting on the Republican side—in Manchuria in 1939 during the heavy fighting at Khalkin Gol between the Soviet Union and Japan, in Finland in 1939–40, and in Poland in 1939. This combat experience indicated the advantages of sloping armor, one of the distinctive features of the T-34

By December 1939, the Soviet Union had developed two new tanks, the KV-1 heavy tank and the T-34 medium tank, the latter arguably the single most influential tank design in the history of armored warfare. The T-34 was designed at the Kharkov Works by Mikhail Koshkin and his team as a replacement for the BT series. It incorporated features from a number of experimental vehicles, including sloping armor from the wheel/track A-20, the 76.2mm gun from subsequent A-30 and a purely tracked variant, the T-32. The first prototypes of the final variant, the T-34, emerged in January 1940, and mass production began in the following June.

The T-34 represented an ideal balance between mobility, protection, and firepower and was the model for much subsequent tank design. Employing modified Christie suspension with wide tracks which reduced ground pressure to a minimum, the T-34 could maintain high speeds even over rough terrain and remain mobile in mud or snow, two elements which were subsequently to dominate on the Eastern Front in World War II. The T-34's hull overhung the tracks and had sloped sides, with the 45mm

glacis laid back at an angle of 60 degrees, conferring the same ballistic protection as a 90mm plate. Dubbed *Prinadlezhit-Cheterviki*, or "34" by its crews, the tank was a weapon of such basic excellence that it was to fight throughout World War II without major modification.

In World War I, Germany had failed to develop a successful tank, and after the 1919 Treaty of Versailles the Germans were forbidden from possessing any tanks at all. However, in the interwar years Germany produced the single most influential advocate of armored warfare, Heinz Guderian.

Guderian had served as a staff officer in World War I. In postwar Germany he became first a signals, then a motor transport specialist, and finally, by way of reading Liddell Hart, an advocate of armored warfare. By the late 1920s he was conducting exercises with dummy tanks and systematically exploring "the possibilities of the tank as a unit, of the tank platoon, the tank company, and the tank battalion." He was beginning to evolve his own theory of the tank as the primary weapon in all-arms formations which allowed it to fight to its full effect, in Panzer (armored) divisions and later corps.

In 1933, during maneuvers at Kummersdorf, Guderian was able to mount a demonstration of experimental PzKpfw. I (*Panzerkampfwagen* I) light tanks for the German Chancellor Adolf Hitler. The Führer was impressed, declaring "That's what I want!" and thus setting the seal

ABOVE RIGHT: *Based on the Renault FT17, the first American tank to be produced in quantity was the M1917 Six-Ton Tank with a total of 950. Here, students at the U.S. Army Tank School at Fort Meade, Maryland put their M1917 "Baby Tanks" through their paces on April 21, 1932.*

RIGHT: *In 1932, General Douglas MacArthur became the Army Chief of Staff and he instituted a full mechanization program for the U.S. Army but it was not until February 1943 that the 1st Cavalry Division finally gave up their horses. Here, cavalry troopers exercise with an M3 Scout Car.*

FAR RIGHT: *The Medium Tank M2 was standardized in June 1939 but by then it was technically obsolete as compared to contemporary models of the German PzKpfw. III and IV. Armed with a 37mm gun and up to eight machine guns, it became the basis for the Medium Tank M3 Grant and Lee series that saw widespread service in World War II.*

on the rapid development of the armored idea within a Germany which was now rearming.

The two-man PzKpfw. I had been designed as a light training vehicle, and volume production began in the summer of 1934. The underpowered Model A was quickly replaced by the more powerful B, with a 100hp Maybach engine accommodating a longer hull and armed with two 7.92mm MG34 machine guns. The driver and commander shared the same fighting compartment, the former climbing in through a hull door in the tank's side and the latter using a hatch in the turret roof. The commander's vision was very restricted when the tank was closed down, and he was obliged to spend much of his time in an exposed in a standing position.

The PzKpfw. I underwent its baptism of fire with the Spanish Nationalists and the Condor Legion in the Spanish Civil War, when some were fitted with a 20mm cannon to boost its meager firepower. Subsequently, it fought in Poland, France, and the Low Countries and then in the Balkans and the Soviet Union. However, by 1940 the PzKpfw. I was vulnerable even to such feeble antitank weapons as the British 2pdr, and its usefulness for all but the most minor tasks was almost exhausted. It was also used as a command tank, self-propelled (SP) antitank gun, ammunition carrier, and, shorn of its turret and powered by wood gas, as a training vehicle.

On October 15, 1935, the German Army formed three Panzer divisions. That year also saw the completion by MAN of the first production models of the three-man PzKpfw. II. The third variant, the Ausf. C, appeared in 1937, carrying thicker frontal armor and main armament of one 2cm KwK 38 gun and coaxial 7.92mm machine gun. By 1939, there were approximately 1,000 PzKpfw. IIs on the strength of the German Army, the mainstay of its armored divisions.

In 1937, the year which saw the arrival of the PzKpfw. II Ausf. D, Guderian published a seminal Book, *Achtung Panzer!*, in which he outlined the future development of Germany's armored forces. Guderian deliberately sought a wide readership, to stimulate interest among the general public and also to counter the arguments against his theories raised by opponents within the German Army. Far from carrying the day unopposed, Guderian's approach, which was to be embodied in the German doctrine of Blitzkrieg, was to remain a subject of fierce debate.

In 1938, Guderian was appointed Chief of Mobile Forces, embracing both armored and motorized troops. In 1939, the German Army took delivery of the PzKpfw. III

Ausf. E mounting a 3.7cm KwK L/45 gun firing both HE and AP for use against other tanks and two 7.92mm machine guns with one in the front hull. The PzKpfw. III had a large turret, which would enable it to be up-gunned in World War II, thus prolonging its useful life. The "dustbin" cupola at the rear of the turret gave the commander an excellent view, the crew layout was roomy and the 320hp Maybach engine ensured adequate cross-country performance. In the first two years of the war a rolling program of modifications added strengthened armor and improved tracks to bear extra weight. By 1941, when Germany invaded the Soviet Union, there were approximately 1,500 PzKpfw. IIIs in service with the German Army.

The only German tank to remain in service throughout the war was the PzKpfw. IV medium tank whose origins lay in a specification of 1935 for a tank to support the PzKpfw. III carrying a large-calibre gun capable of firing a destructive HE shell. The main armament of the PzKpfw. IV was a short-barreled 7.5cm KwK. The layout of the resulting tank closely resembled that of the PzKpfw. III, and it began to arrive in quantity in 1939 in the form of the Ausf. D, which took part in the campaign in Poland in September 1939.

LEFT, TOP TO BOTTOM: *During the 1930s, the U.S. Army produced a series of light tanks that culminated in the famous M3 and M5 Stuart tanks of World War II fame. Fast and reliable, the M3 was the most numerous tank in the U.S. Army up until World War II. Early models were armed with a 37mm main gun and five machine guns with two in side sponsons firing forward.*

WORLD WAR II

Blitzkrieg

It took Germany just 36 days to overcome the Poles. In command of XIX Panzer Corps was General Heinz Guderian. On September 5, Guderian had been greeted by Hitler on the road to Plevno. Gazing at a smashed Polish artillery battery, the Führer reflected, "Our bombers did that!" Guderian was able to correct him: "No, it was our Panzers!"

Armored and motorized infantry divisions had made up some 25 percent of the invasion force, fighting with infantry armies in formations no bigger than corps size. Thus there had been little or no concentration of armor along the lines advocated before the war by Liddell Hart and his German disciple Guderian. Although the armored and mechanized acted as the spearheads of three of the five German armies involved, they were intended to cooperate closely with the infantry formations to which they were attached, rather than operate independently.

RIGHT: *Following the occupation of Czechoslovakia, the Wehrmacht adopted the standard Czech light tank in large numbers. Originally designated the LT-35, the Germans classified it as the PzKpfw. 38 (t) and production of the vehicle continued until 1942. Here, a PzKpfw. IV Ausf. D acts in support of a formation of PzKpfw. 38 (t) light tanks during the invasion of France in 1940.*

LEFT: *Denied the use of tanks by the Versailles Treaty of 1919, the German army developed tanks in secret. The first model to appear was the PzKpfw. I in 1934. Armed with a pair of machine gun, the PzKpfw. I was only suitable as a training vehicle or for displays such as these PzKpfw. I Ausf. B models at a Nazi rally in Nuremberg, although they did see action in Spain and during the early Blitzkrieg campaigns of World War II.*

INSET, LEFT: *The PzKpfw. II entered service in 1935 and was armed with a 20mm cannon and coaxial machine gun. These PzKpfw. II Ausf. A models are shown during the invasion of Czechoslovakia in March 1939.*

LEFT: *The Polish campaign of September 1939 gave rise to the term Blitzkrieg or Lightning War based on the combination of fast moving tanks and armored infantry with overwhelming air support provided by Stuka dive bombers. In reality, the vast majority of the German army relied on such basic forms of transport as the horse and the bicycle for its mobility and this was to remain so for much of the war.*

BELOW: *With a Nazi flag over its engine decks acting as an air-recognition signal, a PzKpfw. II Ausf. A follows a line of PzKpfw. 38 (t) light tanks of the 7th Panzer Division through the rolling countryside of France.*

INSET: *Major General Heinz Guderian was one of the leading lights in the creation of the Wehrmacht's armored forces. During the battle for France in 1940 he commanded the XIX Panzer Corps and is shown here in his command vehicle during the campaign.*

Nevertheless, the armored and mechanized formations played an important role in German victory. And the new concept of *Blitzkrieg* (lightning war) was demonstrated at a tactical level by Guderian's corps which in one sustained burst advanced 50 miles in 12 hours.

This was too much for the largely unmechanized Polish Army, which moved by horses and foot and fielded only a handful of tanks. Nor did it matter that of the 2,800 tanks and armored vehicles fielded by the Germans, only about 300 were battleworthy medium types. Working in close cooperation with artillery, infantry, and dive-bombers the German armor was able to brush aside Polish opposition and pour through gaps into the enemy's rear. In this they were helped by the Polish dispositions, which allowed many of their divisions to be encircled in the first four days of the campaign within 50 miles of their frontier. During the course of the campaign only a few German formations were obliged to cover more than 200 miles.

In May 1940, the French and the British were almost as obliging. The Allies expected a German attack to repeat the so-called Schlieffen Plan of 1914, falling on their left flank as it had in the first summer of World War I. Their right flank was protected by the Maginot Line, and they regarded

ABOVE RIGHT: *The A11 Infantry Tank Mk. I or Matilda I was a legacy of the Great War when tanks acted as infantry support weapons. This doctrine continued into World War II in British tank manufacture. Although well armored, the Matilda I was only armed with a single .50cal machine gun and so was unable to fight other tanks*

RIGHT: *The Char B1-bis was the principal French heavy tank in 1940. Weighing 32 tons it was armed with a 75mm gun in the hull and a 47mm gun in the turret.*

OPPOSITE, ABOVE LEFT: *A PzKpfw. 38 (t) of the 7th Panzer Division lies burned out and abandoned after being destroyed by French antitank guns on May 27, 1940.*

OPPOSITE, BELOW LEFT: *Knocked-out German and French armored vehicles lie scattered along the main road leading into Le Cateau after fierce fighting that took place there during the fall of France.*

OPPOSITE, RIGHT: *The French Char B1-Bis was more powerful than any tank fielded by the Germans in 1940. With an infinitely variable steering system, the 75mm gun in the hull could be trained with precision while the 47mm in the fully rotating turret was a more potent antitank weapon than the 37mm of the PzKpfw. III or 38 (t) of the time.*

Panzertruppen of the 7th Panzer Division rearm and refuel their Czech-built PzKpfw. 38 (t) light tanks during the battle for France in May 1940. The hull of the PzKpfw. 38 (t) subsequently became the basis for several successful self-propelled weapons such as the Bison and the Hetzer.

INSET: A column of A9 cruiser tanks of 1st Royal Tank Regiment, 7th Armoured Division passes along an Egyptian street during the early days of the North African campaign in May 1940. The Cruiser Tank Mk. I was the first in a line of decidedly indifferent British tank designs that constantly lagged behind contemporary German models.

the wooded and hilly Ardennes, in the center of their line, as untankable.

The Germans gave them what they expected. German Army Group B advanced through Holland and Belgium, drawing the Allied left flank forward. Simultaneously, Army Group A drove through the uncovered Ardennes, cutting the Allied armies in two.

Army Group A contained ten Panzer divisions, their force multiplied by close support from the Luftwaffe. This was critical to the success of the German armor at the critical point of the German drive in the West as, tank for tank, the German vehicles were not significantly superior to those of the British and French armies. The PzKpfw. IV was well armored but undergunned. The PzKpfw. III, the German Army's workhorse in 1940, was not as well armored as the British Infantry Tank Matilda Mk. I and Mk. II and the French Char B1 and SOMUA S-35. What tipped the balance, however, was that the German Panzer divisions were unencumbered by infantry and artillery, and trained to maximize their tank's primary characteristics of speed, maneuverability, and independence of action.

In contrast, the British Expeditionary Force in France fielded only one armored division, 1st Armoured, which was in the process of forming. The French had plenty of tanks (3,000 to the overall German figure of 2,400) but had parceled out half of them to their infantry divisions, frittered away another 700 to so-called "cavalry" and "mechanized" formations and retained only 800 to form armored divisions proper. In the early summer of 1940 only three were active and one, under General Charles de Gaulle, was still forming.

RIGHT: *The Valentine Infantry Tank Mk. III was produced in greater numbers than any other British tank, with 6,855 being built in Britain with a further 1,420 being manufactured in Canada. The Valentine was subsequently converted to several other roles—such as the DD amphibious tank and as the basis of the Bishop and Archer self-propelled weapons*

FAR RIGHT: *The British Army employed "tankettes" in large numbers for policing the far-flung reaches of the British Empire. They were cheap to produce and simple to operate, as well as being sufficiently intimidating against hostile natives. Here, a Vickers Light Tank Mk. VIB leads a column of Universal Carriers during a training exercise.*

ABOVE: *A South African Mk. III reconnaissance car leads a pair of Marmon-Herrington Mk. II armored cars into Benghazi. These armored cars were manufactured in South Africa and served with success during the North African campaign. Both of these models were armed with a Boys antitank rifle and up to three machine guns*

RIGHT: *Members of the 8th Hussars parade with their Vickers Light Tanks Mk. VIA at Helmiya in Egypt on June 5, 1940. The Vickers light tank series formed the bulk of the British Royal Armoured Corps at the outbreak of World War II.*

On the other side, the German armored divisions were homogenous and subordinated to higher Panzer headquarters. They were the largest armored force existing in any army, enjoying excellent radio communications. They were the forerunners of the great tank armies which would dominate the battlefields of the Eastern Front, Western Desert, and Northwest Europe.

The German offensive was launched on May 10, and two days later Army Group A had forced its way through the Ardennes and reached the River Meuse. Three bridgeheads across the Meuse were established in the next two days and a 50-mile front was driven west between Sedan and Dinant. By May 20, German tanks had reached the Channel at Noyelles, severing communications between the French and the British, who were falling back from Belgium with their rear now threatened by Guderian's XIX Panzer Corps.

On May 21 the British launched a counterattack at Arras, attempting to link with French forces to the south. Mounted by infantry from 50th Division and 74 Matilda infantry tanks (58 Mk. Is, 16 Mk. IIs) and a handful of French armored units, the hastily assembled counterstroke was led by Maj-Gen G. le Q. Martel, a leading advocate of armor during the interwar years.

The counterattack was brought to a halt and then turned back after an advance of six miles. But it had taken 400 prisoners and delivered a rude shock to the German 7th Panzer Division commanded by General Erwin Rommel. It was the British Army's first major battle of the war and it had cost them 32 Mk. Is and two Mk. IIs, many of them destroyed by 88mm antiaircraft guns operating in antitank role. The "88" was to prove a formidable tank-stopper. In the desert battles of Sidi Rezegh and Gazala, from November 1941 to June 1942, Rommel fashioned tactics where he engaged British tanks before drawing them on to a screen of antitank guns, only advancing again when the losses they had inflicted had deprived the British of the means to mount a mobile defense.

The brief action at Arras exercized a crucial influence over the commander of Army Group A, Field Marshal Gerd von Rundstedt who, overanxious about German losses, ordered his tanks to halt on the eve they were poised to seize the port of Dunkirk. The subsequent British and French evacuation saved over 300,000 troops but not their armor. In the "miracle" of Dunkirk 1st Armored Division left almost all of its A9 Cruiser tanks in France.

After the fall of France the Germans took over many of the French Army's tanks. Some of the Hotchkiss light tanks, equipped with radio and a new cupola, were later used on the Eastern Front. The Char B1 was used in a variety of roles, including those of training tank and an SP model mounting a 105mm howitzer.

In the invasion of the Soviet Union in June 1941, Operation "Barbarossa," the German Army fielded 17 Panzer divisions in three Panzer groups, a total of 3,322 armored fighting vehicles. In the Soviet Union the battles of encirclement (*Kesselschlacht*) which had characterized the campaign in Poland were repeated on a massive scale. As in Poland, the Soviets moved a significant proportion of their forces up to the border, inviting rapid encirclement. The Panzer groups raced ahead along a front of nearly 1,000 miles, carving out nine major and 13 smaller encirclements which were in turn reduced by the German infantry as the Panzers moved further into the Russian heartland and on toward Moscow. In all, these encirclements yielded nearly three million prisoners, 14,000 tanks (of the approximately 24,000 fielded by the Red Army at the start of "Barbarossa") and 25,000 guns—the equivalent of 150 divisions. German losses between June and November amounted to some 80,000 men and 2,300 tanks.

"Barbarossa" came to halt before Moscow at the beginning of December 1941, denied the Soviet capital by the mud of the autumn rainy season, the onset of the winter snow, and the arrival of Red Army reinforcements rushed from the

RIGHT: *The pitiful performance of British cruiser tanks in the first years of World War II led to an urgent demand for improved models. Manufacture of the Medium Tank M3 began in April 1941 and it was supplied to the British under the Lend-Lease Act. There were two basic types of the M3 which in British service were named the Lee and the Grant after the famous generals of the American Civil War. The Lee featured the original turret while the Grant had a British-designed version.*

In the Western Desert a tank was not just a fighting vehicle but a home as well. Crews carried all manner of items to make their nomadic life more bearable. This Vickers Mk. VIB light tank belonged to Col W.G. Petherick, the commanding officer of the 3rd Hussars during the winter of 1940.

ABOVE: *After the collapse of the Italian army in North Africa at the hands of the Desert Rats, Hitler despatched the Deutsches Afrika Korps in support of his fascist ally, Benito Mussolini. Vehicles of the Afrika Korps are unloaded in Tripoli harbor while the Italian officers loiter the foreground feigning indifference.*

BELOW: *A PzKpfw. III Ausf. F passes a disabled Infantry Tank Mk. IIA Matilda II. Armed with a 50mm main gun, the PzKpfw. III was the principal tank of the Afrika Korps in the early battles with the British Eighth Army.*

ABOVE: *The M3 light tank was manufactured in several versions with the early models of all-riveted construction until superseded by all-welded models with a cast turret such as this one. With a weight of 12.3 tons, the M3 had a top speed of 35mph and a four-man crew.*

BELOW: *The Medium Tank M4 was standardized in October 1941. It was named the Sherman and early production models, as shown here, featured a welded hull with a three-piece bolted differential housing at the front and a 75mm gun in a narrow M34 gun mount.*

The British armored doctrine of deploying two types of tanks—cruiser and infantry—was flawed and wasted scant resources on too many different designs. Here, an Infantry Tank Mk. III undertakes an exercise with accompanying infantry in North Africa during April 1943 by when the tank was obsolete.

east. Infantry and armor were at the end of their tether, and the latter had encountered for the first time a formidable new opponent which was to become a vital factor on the Eastern Front.

The War-Winning T-34

By June 1941, the Red Army had received a total of 1,225 T-34s, and by the Battle of Moscow another 1,858 had arrived at frontline units, many of which were chewed up in "Barbarossa." Nevertheless, the appearance on the battlefield of the T-34 came as a great surprise to the Germans, who rapidly came to appreciate its all-round excellence.

In true Soviet style, the T-34 made few concessions to crew comfort. Initially, it lacked a radio and a turret with an all-round sight for its commander, but remained a superb fighting machine. It had a crew of four: the driver/hull gunner, who sat in the forward part of the tank, the latter operating the T-34's 7.62mm machine-gun; and the turret crew of loader and commander (who also doubled as the gunner) laying and firing the gun in a cramped turret. The commander and loader sat on padded seats mounted on a tubular support, each provided with a wide cushioned backrest fitted to the turret ring. Since the turret crew's seats were themselves attached to the turret ring, they did not revolve with the gun as the turret traversed, obliging both loader and commander to squirm in their seats as the gun swung around.

In battle the T-34's commander had his work cut out, shouting directions by microphone to the driver, who had only a restricted frontal view, bellowing orders to the loader as to the type of ammunition he wanted, ducking down to the periscope or cranked telescope sight to lay the gun, working out the range, opening fire and then keeping himself well clear of the of the 76.2mm gun as it lunged back for a full 14 inches on recoil. This left him little time to see what other tanks in his formation were doing. By using a hand trigger attached to the main armament to fire the gun, rather than the spring-mounted foot pedal bolted to the gun mounting, the overworked commander could remain in the turret for longer periods.

Life was further complicated by an electric-powered traverse which frequently broke down, requiring the commander/gunner to haul the heavy turret round with a manually operated traverse so awkwardly placed that that it contorted him into a crouching position, his right hand stretched across his body, cranking away, while he strove to keep his head firmly pressed against the sight's rubber eyeguard which let in distracting amounts of light.

The loader also had his problems. Of the 77 rounds carried by the T-34 (on average 19 rounds AP and 53 HE plus five shrapnel) only nine were immediately accessible—six in racks on the left-hand wall of the fighting compartment and three on the right. The remaining 69 rounds were distributed in eight metal bins at the bottom of the turret, covered by rubber matting which formed the turret floor. In any action in which more than a handful of rounds were fired without an appreciable pause, the loader had to start uncovering and dismantling the turret floor in order to replenish the gun. Struggling amid a tangle of bins and matting, he faced an extra hazard every time the gun was fired, discharging a burning hot shell case into the debris.

These drawbacks were outweighed by the T-34's rugged all-weather engine, modified Christie suspension, and broad tracks. Its sloping armor increased resistance to shell penetration and the long-barreled high-velocity 76.2mm gun completed a well-balanced design which combined the basic requirements of firepower, mobility, protection and facilitated rapid mass production and easy repair and maintenance in the field. In the T-34/76 and its successor, the T-34/85 (upgunned to 85mm),

ABOVE RIGHT: Tank crews of the 8th King's Royal Irish Hussars confer in the desert with their M3 light tanks in the background. Officially named the Stuart by the British, crews nicknamed it the "Honey" due to its high mobility and reliability as compared to most British tanks of the time.

RIGHT: An A9 Cruiser Tank Mk. I kicks up the dust in the Western Desert. Armed with a 2pdr main armament with a coaxial machine gun and two auxiliary machine gun turrets each side of the driver's position, the A9 was undergunned, too thinly armored, and mechanically unreliable.

FAR RIGHT: Once a gun tank became obsolete, it was common practice to use the hull and automotive components for other purposes such as this Carrier, Valentine, 25pdr Gun Mk. I as shown here firing on enemy positions in Tunisia, May 1943. In the foreground, under the camouflage netting, is the ammunition limber for the 25pdr gun.

which entered production in the winter of 1943, the Red Army had a war winner.

The T-34 was to account for nearly 70 percent of all Soviet tank production. In the field it was supported by the KV-1 heavy tank, which was also armed with a 76.2mm gun. During the summer of 1942, a lighter, faster version, the KV-1S was introduced, to be followed in the summer of 1943 by the more heavily armored and armed KV-85, which carried an 85mm gun.

The German Response—the Tiger I

The T-34 was to bring about a profound change in tank design. At first serious consideration was given to producing a German copy, which would incorporate universal radio installation and powered turret traverse. The designers demurred, however, not solely from wounded pride but also because of the technical difficulties involved in manufacturing the aluminum components in the diesel engine. Having ruled out military plagiarism, the decision was taken to continue with the development of a 60-ton heavy battle tank, the PzKpfw. Tiger I, which had entered production in the summer of 1942, and to design a lighter tank, the PzKpfw. V Panther, weighing 45 tons, which would incorporated the outstanding features of the T-34.

The origins of the Tiger lay in a 1937 specification for a heavy "breakthrough" tank. But in 1941, following the first encounters with the T-34, the 1937 concept was revived, producing a specification for a heavy tank capable of mounting the formidable 88mm high-velocity gun in a turret with a full traverse and carrying sufficient armor to defeat all present and future antitank weapons.

The development of the Tiger, a competition between Henschel and Dr. Ferdinand Porsche, the brilliant racing car designer, went hand-in-hand with the German artillery arm's demands for powerful self-propelled tank destroyers (*Jagdpanzer*) to supersede the obsolescent 37mm and 50mm towed antitank guns which were proving ineffective against the T-34. Improvised first-generation tank destroyers—Marders—had appeared in 1942, consisting of a 75mm antitank gun mounted on obsolete chassis—PzKpfw. IIs or Czech 38 (t)s. The fighting compartment was protected by a fixed, open-topped superstructure of armor plate. Hitler immediately grasped that the production of Jagdpanzer was not only quicker and cheaper than that of tanks but that it also provided a fast track to boosting the strength of the Panzer arm. In this he received the partisan encouragement of the artillery arm, which had been careful to retain the assault guns and tank destroyers within its command.

From this jockeying for position emerged the Elefant, a Jagdpanzer variant based on one of Porsche's prototype Tiger chassis, which carried an 88mm gun on a fixed superstructure at the rear of the hull and was protected at the front by 200mm of armor plate. At first sight the Elefant was a formidable beast, but in comparison with the improvized Marder it was expensive to produce. It also shared the Marder's limitation of a narrow field of fire and restricted accommodation. Furthermore, it lacked secondary armament. On the Eastern Front, the 90 Elefants which were committed to the Kursk offensive in July 1943, were highly vulnerable to Red Army tank-hunting parties. The survivors were fitted with machine guns and despatched to serve in a semi-static role in Italy, where their heavy armor proved all but impervious to Allied antitank guns.

Porsche lost the battle with Henschel, whose Tiger I was committed to battle in August-September 1942. Like the Mk. Is in 1916, it was thrown into action piecemeal, rather than en masse and in favorable conditions. The first small batch of Tigers went into action in secondary operations in the swampy forests near Leningrad where the terrain was quite unsuitable. Lumbering in single file along the forest tracks, the Tigers were picked off by Red Army antitank gunners.

Nevertheless, the Tiger emerged from this discouraging combat debut as the most powerful tank in the world. Its 88mm gun, which had 92 rounds of ammunition, packed a heavy punch and outranged the T-34. Its armor was not well sloped, but it was 100mm thick at the front and 80mm thick around the sides. The Tiger's weight made it slow, however, with a cross-country speed of only 12mph, which limited its operational radius to about 60 miles and imposed severe strain on its gearbox. By November 1942, production of Tigers had reached 25 a month.

Tigers equipped heavy tank battalions which were usually at the disposal of Panzer corps commanders.

New Methods of Tank Operations

In 1941, Operation "Barbarossa" had caught the Red Army cold in the middle of the reorganization of its tank arm. In spring 1942, it activated 12 tank corps and two tank armies. Commander of VII Tank Corps, an element of Fifth Tank Army, was a rising star of Soviet mechanized operations, General Pavel Rotmistrov. In the fighting around Voronezh, Rostov, and Stalingrad, Rotmistrov began to formulate a method of tank operations based on a high degree of mobility and powerful, direct, active maneuver. However, Fifth Tank Army was at the time no more than an infantry army with a strong armored element, comprising two tank corps, six rifle divisions, a cavalry corps, an independent tank brigade (of approximately 50 tanks), a motorcycle regiment, and artillery.

Rotmistrov was convinced that the mixture of tanks and infantry was a mistaken policy and that the future lay with all-tank armies, combining one or two tank corps with a mechanized corps. Early in 1943, Stalin was persuaded to authorize the creation of five tank armies proper. One of them, Fifth Guards, was to be commanded by Rotmistrov.

Fifth Guards Tank Army was to play a key role in the Battle of Kursk in July 1943, a pivotal moment in the story of armored warfare in World War II. By summer 1943, the tank was no longer the autonomous battle-winner it had been in France in summer 1940, when infantry fled at the mere rumor of the approach of armor. The intervening two years had seen the development of effective antitank measures which enabled infantry to stand their ground when threatened with armored attack.

Nor was the tank cast in the role of independent spearhead but rather one element in an all-arms battle in which infantry, artillery, and air strikes all played their part. The Battle of Kursk was itself an extraordinary throwback which recalled 1918—a gigantic battle of attrition in which German armor attempted to "pinch off" a massively defended salient in the center of the

Red Army line. There was no room for breakneck maneuver as the armored tips of the German twin attacks stuck fast in a carefully prepared killing ground laced with minefields and criss-crossed with linked fire positions and trench systems which would have sent a chill down the spine of any veteran of summer 1917.

When the German Fourth Panzer Army's II SS Panzer Corps threatened to break through the southern face of the salient and into open country, its advance was halted on July 10 at Prokhorovka by the arrival of Rotmistrov and Fifth Guards Tank Army, rushed up from the Red Army reserve. The encounter produced one of the most remarkable tank clashes of the war, a vast armored brawl fought at pointblank range by some 700 AFVs of II SS Panzer Corps and approximately 850 from Fifth Guards Tank Army. Rotmistrov's tank formations took heavy losses but stopped the Panzers in their tracks. It was the beginning of the end for the Panzer arm.

Kursk also marked the beginning of the combat career a new German medium tank, the five-man 45-ton PzKpfw. V Panther. Developed by Maschinen-fabrik Augsburg-Nürnberg in response to the threat posed by the T-34, the Panther entered production in November 1942 and incorporated its rival's most notable features, including a sloped glacis and wide tracks, and mounting a 75mm L/70 gun and two 7.92mm machine guns. However, the penalty paid for designing and developing the Panther at such speed was an initial mechanical unreliability which produced frequent engine fires. Small numbers were sent into action at Kursk—in spite of the protests of General Guderian, the Inspector of Armored Troops—and most of them broke down before they reached their start lines.

The Panther's teething troubles were quickly overcome and it acquired a formidable reputa-

LEFT: *British and American reconnaissance troops pause to confer on the road to Rome. The British are in a Universal Carrier while the Americans are mounted in an M5 light tank and six-wheeled M8 armored cars.*

RIGHT: *The Germans initiated the use of half-track vehicles for their armored infantry and the Allies soon copied the idea with the Carrier, Personnel, Half-Track, M3. Here, a crewman engages the enemy with his pedestal-mounted .50cal heavy machine gun.*

American armored doctrine decreed that the task of engaging enemy tanks was the particular role of a specialized AFV known as a tank destroyer (TD). These commonly mounted in an open-topped turret a heavier weapon than the standard gun tank. This M10 gun motor carriage is negotiating a narrow street in Artena, Italy.

tion. Eventually some 5,500 were produced, of which 3,740 were the Model G. The tank's most notable derivative was the Jagdpanther tank destroyer, which was armed with an 88mm L/71 Pak 43/3 gun and entered service in 1944.

At Kursk the Germans had pitted some 2,400 tanks and assault guns against the Red Army's 3,300. Both sides suffered losses of about 1,500 AFVs, but the Soviets, whose major war plants had been relocated east of the Urals in 1941, and out of range of German bombers, were better able to take this setback in their stride. The 29,000 tanks which rolled off Soviet production lines in 1944 were deployed on only one front, whereas Germany's equivalent armored output of 29,600 had—from summer 1944—to fight on three. The Third Reich was now fighting a defensive war, and this strategic shift was reflected in the fortunes of its tank arm. However, at a tactical level, superior battlefield reflexes of German crews could still carry the day against the rigid tactics employed by their Soviet counterparts.

The campaign in the east had seen the rise of tank "aces" like Lt Michael Wittmann, who had won an Iron Cross First Class with the SS Leibstandarte Division at Rostov, where his Tiger destroyed six Red Army tanks in a single action. At Kursk, Wittmann's Tiger had fought in the Leibstandarte's heavy Panzer company concentrated in the tip of a wedge formation, the so-called *Panzerkeil*, in which Wittmann fought alongside tank commanders who were fellow-aces, men with a special ability to destroy enemy armor. These armor-clad *Experten* (experts) were the army equivalents of the Luftwaffe's Eastern Front fighter aces such as Erich "Bubi" Hartmann (352 victories). They could instinctively read any tactical situation, and had a sixth sense for the likely movements of enemy vehicles. To this they added a coolness under attack which enabled them to hold their fire until the last possible moment; and, perhaps the most important of all, they fought with highly trained and experienced crews who were able to anticipate their commander's orders. In Balthasar Woll, Wittmann possessed a gunner who had an almost supernatural ability to fire accurately

LEFT: *The M10 Gun Motor Carriage mounted a 3-inch gun in an open turret mounted on a modified Sherman chassis. The M10 was also used by the British under the designation "3-inch SP Wolverine."*

ABOVE: *After they were superseded by the M4 Sherman in North Africa, many M3 Lee and Grant medium tanks were despatched to the Far East for service with the Australian, Indian, and British armored regiments fighting the Japanese. With little armored opposition the M3 proved to be an effective infantry support weapon with its hull-mounted 75mm gun.*

while on the move. On July 5, 1943, the first day of the Battle of Kursk, Wittmann claimed eight enemy tanks knocked out and seven antitank guns destroyed.

At this level, experienced German tank crews still enjoyed a freedom denied their opponents, whom one German tank commander likened to "herds of buffalo menaced by leopards." But even this local advantage could be frittered away. The Panzerkeil tactic itself was criticized for placing the relatively slow-moving Tiger at its head. The Tiger was at its most potent when standing off the T-34 and engaging the lighter tank at range with its 88mm gun. It lost its advantage in close-quarter combat where the T-34's maneuverability and strength in numbers offset the formidable armor and armament of the Tiger.

At a strategic level, the German Panzer arm had also to contend with the reduction of the number of fighting machines in the field. Its armored divisions had originally been designed to contain four tank battalions with a total strength of approximately 400 tanks per division. By the beginning of 1943, there were only three battalions in a division, one of which was quipped with tank destroyers (Jagdpanzer). Matters were complicated by the withdrawal of the obsolete PzKpfw. II and the difficulty that commanders of old formations faced when attempting to secure allocations of new tanks which were reserved for the building up of fresh divisions to satisfy Hitler's *rage de nombre*, his obsession with the quantity of formations rather than their quality.

The reluctance of these commanders to send back vehicles in need of major overhaul to Germany also meant that many tanks remained stranded in divisional garages not best equipped to repair them. As a result panzer divisions often mustered fewer than 100 tanks. Firepower was further

LEFT: *The venerable M1917 Six-Ton Tank continued as a driver training vehicle well into World War II and then as a training aid to teach infantrymen close-quarter antitank tactics.*

CENTER LEFT, INSET: *One of the most important weapons in the Allied inventory was the wide range of landing ships developed for amphibious assaults from the sea. Of these the Landing Ship Tank (LST) was fundamental to the Allied victory from the Mediterranean Sea to Normandy. Here, M4A3 medium tanks disgorge from an LST during the Salerno landings in Italy. Standardized in January 1942, the M4A3 Sherman was the production model most favored by the U.S. Army.*

CENTER LEFT: *The Centaur was a specialized antiaircraft tank mounting two 20mm Polsten cannons. This one is shown coming ashore during the landings in Normandy. As the German air threat was negligible, these vehicles were soon withdrawn from service*

BOTTOM LEFT: *The M3 Lee/Grant series featured a variety of different engines but all were robust and reliable. In British service, the machine gun cupola at the commander's position was often removed and a simple hatch substituted.*

RIGHT: *An early production M4 Sherman is put through its paces during training in the United States. The M4 shared many features with its predecessor including the Vertical Volute Spring Suspension and the Continental R-975 400hp air-cooled radial engine that gave the tank a top speed of 24mph.*

BELOW: *The cast hull of the M4A1 model is shown to advantage here as the crew take a break in an Italian town under the watchful gaze of the commander manning the .50cal machine gun. Note the large wine flagon on the mudguard next to the hull-mounted machine gun.*

FAR RIGHT: *M8 armored cars of the 36th Division of the Fifth U.S. Army line up just before boarding an LST at an embarkation port in Italy, May 1944. Known in British service as the Greyhound, the M8 was a highly successful vehicle and was extensively employed in the Italian and Northwest Europe campaigns.*

reduced by the division of authority between the Panzer arm and the artillery, which enabled the latter to draw off the Jagdpanzer for the motorized infantry formations and the Waffen-SS.

After Kursk, which was fought at a level of approximate armored parity, overall German tactical superiority was increasingly offset by the growing numerical superiority, in all arms, enjoyed by the Red Army. The brutal simplicity which the Russians brought to armored warfare was well expressed by General Fridolin Senger und Etterlin, commander of 17th Panzer Division in the winter of 1942–43:

"The Russians had these principles to pick up the best type of machine wherever they could get it; to have only very few types; to construct the type as simply as possible; and then to produce these types in large quantities."

In Germany the precise opposite happened. While events demanded a ruthless standardization of German armor, Hitler's ceaseless meddling with matters of detail resulted in ever wilder flights of fancy: an Elefant equipped with a 210mm mortar; the development of Ram Tigers for street fighting; the transformation of the Gustav 800mm railway gun in an antitank weapon; and, most extraordinary of all, a specification for a 1,000-ton "land monitor," final proof of the galloping gigantism which had overtaken the Führer's military thinking. The result of this manic doodling, when applied to models already in production, was, as Guderian noted, the

"... creation of countless variations to the original type, each of which would need innumerable spare parts. The repair of tanks in the field became impossible."

All this occurred at a time when the USSR was concentrating on the mass-production of the T-34.

LEFT: *During World War II, the United States became the arsenal of democracy and the Lend-Lease scheme bolstered the armies of several nations, in particular Britain, France, and the Soviet Union. The jeep and the 2½-ton truck were fundamental to the Allied victory in mechanized warfare waged on every front. During World War II, the United States provided her allies with sufficient civil and military aid to equip 2,000 infantry divisions.*

In the great offensives of summer 1944, which in their scope and scale matched the envelopments of "Barbarossa," the Red Army enjoyed an overall advantage in tanks of at least 4:1 and was able to achieve an even greater measure of superiority at local level. In its great drive to Berlin, its armored divisions relied on two primary elements: the T-34 and the Dodge truck, the latter supplied through Lend-Lease by the Americans.

U.S. Tank Development

During the interwar years the United States had manufactured only a small amount of military equipment for its own needs. By 1944 it was producing no less than 40 percent of the world's armaments. In 1940 only 346 tanks had been built in the U.S. In 1943–44 47,000 tanks, almost all of them M4 Shermans, were produced—a tribute to the American genius for mass-production. By May 1945 U.S. tank production figures, operating at full throttle and far from the threat of air attack, had reached 88.000 of all types.

The first U.S. tank to be built in any quantity was the 15-ton, four-man M3 light tank, some 6,000 of which had been produced by August 1942, carrying a 37mm main armament and three .303in Browning machine guns. By June 1944, when production ceased some 22,750 Stuarts had been built, of which the M5A1 was the most numerous example (6,810).

The M3 was the first US-built tank to see action with the British Army in World War II. The first Lend-Lease delivery of 84 M3 Stuarts to the Eighth Army arrived in North Africa in July 1941 and in November of that year 163 Stuarts took part in Operation "Crusader," the relief of Tobruk. The M3 subsequently appeared in all theaters of war, becoming the most widely used light tank of World War II, affectionately dubbed the "Honey" by the British. By July 1943, some 13,859 had been built.

Operation "Overlord" was the codename for the allied invasion of Nazi occupied Europe. It was the largest combined operations amphibious landing in the history of warfare. For two years the British and American armies had gathered and trained until southern England became virtually a military camp. In May and early June 1944, this vast conglomeration of war material congregated at English ports for the invasion of Normandy.

By summer 1940, the success of the German Panzer divisions in France had persuaded senior American officers that their medium tanks should be armed with a 75mm gun which would be a match for the PzKpfw. III and IV. As the M4 medium tank, mounting a 75mm gun in fully traversing turret, was not yet ready for quantity production, an interim design was produced based on the M2 infantry tank. The M2's wide hull was used to accommodate a sponson-mounted 75mm gun, with limited traverse, and a 37mm gun was mounted in the turret.

By December 1942, a total of 6,528 M3 Lee medium tanks had been built, with the British placing a substantial order not only for the Lee but also for a variation of its own, the Grant, which had a larger cast turret to conform with the British practice of carrying the tank's radio in the turret, where it was operated by the loader. As a result the Grant carried a crew of six rather than the seven in a Lee.

Both Lees and Grants took part in the battles of Alam Halfa and Alamein and the pursuit of the Axis army to Tunisia. When the British Eighth Army's fortunes had been at their lowest ebb, the Grant was dubbed the "ELH" (Egypt's Last Hope). The ability of their sponson-mounted 75mm guns to fire AP or HE ammunition gave Eighth Army a qualitative advantage over the enemy.

The successor to the stop-gap M3 Lee was the 33-ton M4 Sherman, of which 49,243 had been built when production ceased in June 1945. More Shermans were built than any other single tank in World War II, a tribute to American industry. The Sherman retained the Lee's chassis, engine, transmission, and lower hull but mounted its 75mm main armament in a cast turret with all-round traverse, in the process eliminating the Lee's 37mm gun and reducing the crew to five. By the time the pilot model appeared at the beginning of 1942, the United States was at war and the Sherman went into mass production, ultimately with ten manufacturers, within a few weeks.

Combat experience quickly revealed that the Sherman was undergunned in comparison with the German Tiger and Panther, and later models of the M4A1, M4A2, and M4A3 were armed with a 76mm gun in a redesigned turret which

ABOVE: *A "Rhino" ferry packed with troops and vehicles approaches the Normandy invasion beaches on D-Day, June 6, 1944. By midnight, 57,500 U.S. and 75,000 British and Canadian troops were ashore*

BELOW: *Named Virgin, an M4A4 Sherman together with AEC Matador 3-ton trucks motor on to a "Rhino" ferry barge from U.S. Coast Guard-manned LST-21 during the early hours of the Normandy invasion.*

RIGHT AND BELOW RIGHT: *Two more views of the Normandy beaches. U.S. troops and vehicles stream ashore. M3A1 half-tracks move along the shoreline towing 57mm antitank guns.*

BELOW: *With their prominent white stars readily visible to Allied aircraft, British trucks start the journey across the Channel to the invasion beaches.*

RIGHT: *U.S. troops follow an M4A1 Sherman into action. The close terrain of the "bocage" region of Normandy was ideal terrain for the tenacious German defenders and it took many weeks to break out of the bridgehead.*

BELOW: *Bodies and knocked out vehicles (here an M4 Sherman; note the extended engine air intakes to allow deep water operation) clog the Normandy beaches after the landings. The beach defenses were of minimal value: they helped some attackers hide from the withering German defensive fire.*

ABOVE: Firing the 105mm of an M7 howitzer motor carriage during training in the U.S. The M7 was the marriage of a Sherman chassis and a 105mm howitzer to create an effective self-propelled artillery weapon capable of providing close support to armored formations.

ABOVE LEFT: The "bocage" comprized numerous sunken lanes with thick hedgerows bordering every field. In order to break through these natural defensive obstacles, many American tanks were fitted with a device known as the "Cullin cutter" or "hedgerow device," so named after its inventor. The prongs were made from German beach antitank barriers as shown on this M5 light tank.

LEFT: The M4 Sherman was originally armed with a dual-purpose 75mm gun but it was largely ineffective against the latest generation of German tanks such as the Panther and Tiger I so a larger M1A1 76mm gun was developed mounted in a new turret designated T23 as shown on this M4A1 (76mm) which was known as the Sherman IIA in British service.

FAR LEFT: *The crew of an M4A1 relax as they consume a bunch of grapes during a field exercise. They are all wearing the distinctive U.S. tankers' headgear that was based on an American football protective helmet.*

LEFT: *The crew of an early production M4 medium tank undertake general maintenance on their Sherman in the field. The early production Sherman model featured vision blocks in the hull front for the driver and hull gunner but these were soon deleted to enhance armor integrity over the frontal aspect.*

BELOW: *The M3A1 was an improved model of half-track with an armored housing or "pulpit" for the .50cal machine gun. This version also features a power-assisted winch in the front bumper*

The Hanomag SdKfz. 251 was the standard half-track of the Wehrmacht throughout World War II but it was never produced in sufficient numbers to equip any but the elite formations such as the premier Panzer divisions and the Waffen-SS.

THIS PAGE: *The Tiger I was a truly formidable tank that gained a fearsome reputation among Allied tank crews. The SdKfz. 181 PzKpfw. VI Tiger I Ausf. E was developed by Henschel in response to the success of the Soviet T-34. The Tiger first saw action on the Eastern Front in late 1942. Mounting the highly successful 88mm Flak gun that proved so effective in the anti-tank role, it outgunned all contemporary Allied tank designs and its thick armor made it almost immune to all Allied anti-tank weapons over the frontal aspect at normal combat ranges. However, its weight of 56 tons markedly reduced its overall mobility and made recovery operations difficult in the extreme. Furthermore, its 650hp Maybach engine was not overly reliable and many were lost to mechanical breakdowns rather than combat.*

The later model of the Tiger I PzPpfw. VI Ausf. E. featured all steel resilient road wheels, an improved commander's cupola and uprated engine of 700hp as shown on this Tiger of the 2.Kompanie Schwere SS-Panzer Abteilung 101 during the Normandy campaign.

improved armor-piercing capability but nevertheless fell short of the British Firefly conversion, which had a 17pdr gun. Until the British introduced the A34 Comet cruiser tank in March 1945, the Firefly was the only tank they fielded which was capable of tackling the Tiger and Panther on anything like equal terms.

Active service also revealed that the Sherman had an alarming tendency to "brew up" if penetrated by a shell. To overcome this fault, attempts were made to provide wet stowage for the ammunition, the bins being surrounded by water jackets. This dubious reputation earned it nicknames such as "Ronson" after a cigarette lighter that the makers said, "Lights first time," and with the Germans of "Tommy Cooker."

As well as providing the backbone of the U.S. armored forces, the Sherman was also the mainstay of British armored divisions, which counted on its general reliability in action, ease of maintenance, and sheer weight of numbers to offset its inferiority against the Panther, Tiger, and the fearsome 68-ton Royal Tiger. (This was the SdKfz. 182 PzKpfw. VIB Tiger II, or Königstiger, introduced in autumn 1944 and fitted with Porsche-built turret which mounted an 88mm KwK 43 L/71 gun.) Sherman derivatives included the Skink antiaircraft tank, the M40 tank destroyer, and the "Funnies" (see page 80) such as the DD—Duplex-Drive—swimming tank or the mine-detonating Crab flail tank.

Allied Use of Armor

The first significant deployment of U.S. armor in World War II took place in November 1942, during Operation "Torch," the Allied invasion of North Africa in which two divisions, 2nd and 1st Armored were committed. Subsequently 2nd Armored was held in reserve while 1st Armored

RIGHT: *The Tiger I was well suited to the defensive battles fought by the German Army from 1943 onward. It took a significant toll of Allied tanks on all fronts with its powerful main armament and superior optics. Tank aces such as Michael Wittmann achieved extraordinary tallies of enemy AFVs destroyed, with his personal total being 132 before he was killed with his crew by the Sherman Firefly of Trooper Joe Ekins (the gunner) of No. 3 Troop, A Squadron of the Nottinghamshire Yeomanry in Normandy on August 8, 1944. Allied tank crews worked on the formula that three of their own tanks would be destroyed for each Tiger so it is no surprise that the Tiger was perceived to be such an awesome tank.*

was very roughly handled by the experienced 10th Panzer Division units of the Afrika Korps in the battle of the Kasserine Pass, which set in train a thorough-going reorganization of the U.S. Army's armored divisions.

In 1944, the U.S. Army in Northwest Europe fielded three types of armored formation: armored divisions, separate tank battalions attached to infantry units, and tank destroyer battalions. The American approach to the role of the armored divisions differed sharply from that of their British allies. The British saw the defeat of the enemy's armor as the principal mission of their own armored divisions. The Americans saw the key role of armor as the exploitation of a breakthrough achieved by the infantry, a point of view they shared with the Soviets.

The majority of U.S. armored divisions had three tank battalions equipped with a total of 177 Shermans, a self-propelled tank destroyer battalion, three self-propelled medium artillery battalions, and three battalions of armored infantry carried in half-tracks. They also fielded some 80 light tanks in a reconnaissance role and had general support artillery and range of specialized units, including ordnance, signal, and engineer units, the last also trained to fight as infantry. In comparison, the average strength of a Panzer division now hovered around 85 AFVs and lagged even farther behind in the numbers and quality of its support and specialized units.

In the fighting in Normandy, the German tank and antitank arm was still capable of dealing out heavy punishment to numerically superior Allied formations. On June 13, 1944, while commanding the 2nd Company of SS Heavy Tank Battalion 101, Lt Michael Wittmann almost single-handedly halted the advance of the British 7th Armored Division in a pitched battle at Villers-Bocage.

LEFT: *The Sturmgeschutz series of assault guns based on the chassis of the Panzerkampfwagen III and IV was a cost-effective alternative to the more expensive turreted tank. Three StuGs could be built for the price of two tanks. This is a StuG III Ausf. G and 7,893 were built up to the end of the war.*

FAR LEFT: *For reconnaissance purposes, the German army used a series of armored cars ranging from the Leichter Panzerspähwagen SdKfz. 222 shown here to the heavy eight-wheel SdKfz. 234 Puma. With a crew of three, the SdKfz. 222 weighed 4.8 tons and was armed with a 20mm cannon and a coaxial 7.92mm machine gun.*

LEFT: *Beside armored cars, the German army made extensive use of motorcycle combinations for reconnaissance tasks with the sidecar mounting an MG34 machine gun. Produced by BMW and Zundapp, these versatile vehicles were used throughout the war.*

BELOW: *Weighing 23.9 tons, the 75mm Sturmgeschütz 40 Ausf. G SdKfz. 142/1 or StuG III Ausf. G was produced from the end of 1942 and was based on the PzKpfw. III Ausf. J. This model featured increased frontal armor and a new commander's cupola with all-round vision episcopes. Fighting in combination with the Tiger and other tanks, the Sturmgeschütz proved highly effective in the defensive battles on the Eastern Front where it exacted a fearful toll of Soviet tanks and AFVs.*

It was in the Allied breakout from the Normandy bridgehead in August 1944—Operation "Cobra"—that the British and Americans scored their sole Blitzkrieg triumph of World War II, a penetration of the enemy's front and the subsequent encirclement and destruction of enemy forces beyond the penetration. This had been achieved by the Germans in France in 1940 and then on a grand scale in Russia during the opening phases of "Barbarossa," but these successes were never repeated on a comparable scale and were to be set in reverse by the terrible slogging match at Kursk. Thereafter it was the Red Army, with its destruction of the German Army Group Center in 1944 in Operation "Bagration," which was to emulate the German triumphs of 1940–41.

In Normandy, the ball was set rolling by the foremost American exponent of armored warfare, General George S. Patton, commander of US Third Army, who had pushed his two corps, the westernmost of the Allied armies, down to the bottom of the Cotentin peninsula. Here the German front had already been broken, at Avranches, and in three days of August, Patton's tanks raced 75 miles. Within a week, one of his corps had wheeled left and was in Le Mans. By August 13, Patton was driving north toward Argentan to link with American forces advancing east and British and Canadian forces pushing south to converge on a pocket around Falaise which contained the German Seventh Army, Fifth Panzer Army, and Panzer Group Eberbach.

The pocket shrank as it was subjected to ceaseless Allied artillery and air bombardment, and the gap was finally closed on August 19, although fighting continued to the 21st. Of the approximately 80,000 Germans trapped inside the pocket, an estimated 20,000 escaped and 50,000 surrendered. Amid the wreckage in the pocket the Americans found 380 tanks and self-

RIGHT: *The M8 howitzer motor carriage (HMC) was based on the chassis of the M5A1 light tank. It mounted a 75mm howitzer as a self-propelled artillery weapon. Being such a compact vehicle, the 75mm rounds were carried in a towed ammunition limber. This M8 75 HMC served with Troop E, 106th Cavalry Reconnaissance Squadron and is seen during combat near Karlsbrunn, Germany on February 2, 1945.*

The final wartime model of the Sherman was known as the M4A3E8 or "Easy Eight," although its official designation was the M4A3 (76mm) HVSS. Fitted with a 76mm M1A1C gun in a T23 turret, it featured a new hull front and suspension termed Horizontal Volute Spring Suspension (HVSS) and wider tracks for improved cross-country mobility.

propelled guns, over 700 artillery pieces, and 5,000 vehicles; the British and Canadians found 187 tanks and self-propelled guns, 157 armored cars and armored personnel carriers, 252 artillery pieces, and 2,500 motor vehicles.

Many of the tanks and AFVs that would be developed and see action in the 60 years that followed the Allied invasion of Normandy were based on designs and operational concepts laid down in the latter years of World War II.

The British experience at the disastrous Dieppe raid in 1942 had shown the need for specialized tanks and armored vehicles to breach defenses and clear obstacles.

Dubbed "Funnies," most were based on the versatile Churchill chassis. ARKs—armored ramp carriers—were equipped with folding bridges to span demolished bridges or cross anti-tank ditches. Armored Vehicles Royal Engineers (AVREs), had a 290mm muzzle-loaded demolition gun, which fired a 40lb bomb known, because of its huge size, as the "flying dustbin." AVREs were well capable of pulverizing German concrete defenses, and also carried fascines, huge bundles of brushwood to fill in anti-tank ditches.

Crabs were mine-clearing tanks with at the front a revolving drum which was fitted with weighted chains; these thrashed their way through minefields safely exploding the mines in their path. The Crab concept had already proved its worth at El Alamein breaching Axis mine-fields. Other tanks carried 110yd long rolls of reinforced matting on a huge drum, known as a Bobbin that they unrolled across soft wet sand to give other vehicles traction. The BARV—Beach Armored Recovery Vehicle—was a turretless tank with winches for towing stranded vehicles off the beach. Finally the grim Crocodile and Wasp flamethrowing tank and light armored vehi-cle were capable of drenching enemy positions in up to 400 gallons of flaming sticky fluid at a range of 120yd. In strict secrecy the British had conducted experiments with these specialized tanks against dummy enemy positions built on remote ranges.

As the landing craft started their run in to the shore, they would launch DD, or Duplex Drive Sherman tanks; though some crews asserted that the initials DD actually stood for "Donald

ABOVE AND LEFT: *The Universal Carrier was a peculiarly British vehicle. Essentially a weapons' transport—carrying mortars, machine guns or being used as a gun tractor—it evolved from a long line of scout and cavalry carriers and entered service in 1940 with production continuing until the end of the war. It was armed with a variety of weapons; often, as here, a Bren gun, something that gave rise to the erroneous designation "Bren Gun Carrier."*

FAR LEFT: *For reconnaissance purposes, the German Army used a series of armored cars ranging from the Leichter Panzerspähwagen (light armored car) SdKfz. 222 to the heavy eight-wheel SdKfz. 234 Puma. With a crew of three, the SdKfz. 222 weighed 4.8 tons and was armed with a 20mm cannon and a coaxial 7.92mm machine gun.*

OPPOSITE: *The SdKfz. 222 first appeared in 1938 and was the standard light armored reconnaissance car during the Blitzkrieg period, although it remained in service thruout the war. Finished in the distinctive Panzer grey of the early war years, the four-wheel drive SdKfz. 222 was manufactured by Auto-Union Horch.*

Duck." With high waterproof "skirts," and a drive off the main engine to two propellers, DD tanks could "swim" ashore. Here they would be able to engage enemy bunkers and defenses with their 75mm guns.

The "funnies" had worked in test conditions, but not all had been tested in combat—D-Day would be their debut.

During the fighting in Normandy that followed D-Day, it was quantity that weighed against the Germans: a potential Allied force of 5,300 tanks against 1,500 German tanks. Qualitatively the Germans deployed superb tanks that had been developed during the war on the Eastern Front, such as the Panther, which—as we have seen—was rushed into production during early 1943 as a counter to the Soviet T-34 and made its combat debut at Kursk. After the war the French Army used captured Panthers in their armored formations.

British Tank Design

The only Allied tank in Normandy that could take on the Panther and Tiger I was the British Sherman IFirefly with a 17pdr gun firing a 17lb shell with a muzzle velocity of 2,900ft per second. The hull machine gun was removed to allow the tank to carry more ammunition for its main armament. It was capable of penetrating five inches of armor at 1,000yd. The rate of fire was 10 rounds per minute. The Firefly was instantly recognizable by the 17pdr gun's long overhang and muzzle brake and the extension on the turret rear to accommodate the radio sets.

In Normandy and Northwest Europe the British deployed the Cromwell, a tank that became numerically the most important British-built cruiser tank of World War II. For the first time, British crews had a tank with the reliable Christie suspension, a powerful engine, and an effective gun.

It was with Cromwells that they fought from June 1944 to the end of the war in Europe. Though by the standards of earlier British designs it was a superior tank, its German opponents like the Panther and late models of the PzKpfw. IV, whose design had benefited from experience on the Eastern Front, still had a marked edge in combat.

OPPOSITE: *The M10 GMC tank destroyer was built in two versions: the M10 based on the diesel-powered M4A2 and the M10A1 on the gasoline-powered M4A3. 4,993 M10s were built as against 1,713 M10A1 GMCs and the latter were retained in the U.S. for training purposes while the former were shipped overseas. They first saw combat in Tunisia following the "Torch" landings in November 1942. However, their performance was not totally satisfactory and the tank destroyer (TD) doctrine remained in doubt to the commanders on the ground such as Bradley and Patton. The subsequent campaigns in Sicily and Italy did not resolve the question. On occasions they were highly successful—such as on February 29, 1944, when the M10s of the 601st TD Battalion knocked out 25 Panzers and assault guns. As the long, bitter Italian campaign wore on they increasingly acted as artillery support rather than in their intended role as tank destroyers as the allies moved northwards in a gruesome battle of attrition.*

OPPOSITE, INSET: *After the Normandy campaign, the Cullin hedgerow device fitted to AFVs was usually discarded, but this M10 of the 740th Tank Destroyer Battalion retains its Douglas version as it passes through the French town of Durne on February 24, 1945, with extra sandbag protection against the threat of hand-held antitank weapons.*

BELOW: *With barrage balloons aloft to ward off German aircraft, a British M10 Wolverine comes ashore over the Normandy beaches draped in waterproofing material around the gun mount. In the background is a Churchill AVRE that was designed specifically to destroy pillboxes and field fortifications on the invasion beaches.*

A column of M4A4 Shermans and Universal Carriers waits in the town of Vassy in France for the order to advance. All the Shermans are fitted with supplementary armor along the sides and are festooned with spare tracklinks as a further marginal level of protection. Unusually for British Shermans, this tank retains the original .50cal machine gun at the commander's position.

BELOW: A Royal Military Policeman directs a line of M4A4 Shermans. The crew of this Sherman wear a mixture of British berets and American tankers' helmets, while the tank itself has supplementary armor plates welded to the hull sides covering the ammunition stowage racks and fuel tanks, as well "cheek" armor on the turret front.

The Cromwell brought together a powerful engine, the Meteor and a versatile gun, the 75mm, that could fire both HE and AP ammunition like the US M3 and M4 mediums. The Cromwell was essentially the Centaur with a down-rated version of the Merlin engine that powered the Supermarine Spitfire fighter. The distinctive features of this engine were the curved flame guards covering the exhausts at the rear of the deck. The 75mm gun was a bored out 6pdr (57mm) that had some teething troubles that were only righted by May 1944. Like the A24 and A27L, the Cromwell had a box-shaped turret composed of an inner skin with an outer layer of armor bolted onto it with bolts prominent on the turret exterior.

The Comet was the first British tank that came near to matching the mobility and firepower of the German Panther; it arrived in the field so late in 1945 that it played no significant part in battle. In it, however, one can see the genesis of the successful Centurion tank.

Leyland had taken over production of the A27 Centaur/Cromwell in May 1943 from Birmingham Carriage & Wagon and immediately began to work on designing an improved version. Mechanically and dimensionally it was similar to the A27, however it was armed with a new "compact" version of the 17pdr gun developed by Vickers-Armstrong. It had a shorter barrel and breach and was consequently slightly lighter. It was known as the Vickers HV 75mm (HV—high velocity) and later the 77mm gun. Its performance and penetrative power were only slightly inferior to the original 17pdr and it used the same ammunition.

Back in 1943, the Department of Tank Design was asked to design a new heavy cruiser tank, the A41. It was to have good armor protection, be armed with a 17pdr (76mm) gun and have a good cross-country performance—a high road speed was not considered essential. The first mock-up of the A41 was completed in 1944 and six prototype tanks were completed in early 1945 and sent to Germany but arrived too late to see any combat. The A41 later became known as the Centurion Mk. 1 and the uparmored A41A became the Centurion Mk. 2, both armed with the 17pdr gun.

Throughout its life the Centurion has proved capable of being uparmored and upgunned. The 17pdr was replaced first by the 20pdr and finally by the 105mm L7-series rifled gun. Other improvements carried out during its life included increased fuel capacity, a contrarotating commander's cupola and improved stowage. All British models of the tank used the same basic Meteor petrol engine and transmission. There have probably been more variants of the Centurion than any other post-World War II MBT.

When production ceased in 1962, 4,423 Centurion tanks had been built, of which at least 2,500 had been exported. The Centurion had enjoyed a distinguished history, seeing action in Korea and Egypt with British forces, with the South African Army, in the Indo-Pakistan wars of 1965 and 1971, the Middle East in 1967 and 1973 with Israeli forces, and in Vietnam with the Australian Army. The Centurion AVRE had been deployed in Northern Ireland in Operation "Motorman," a Beach Armored Recovery Vehicle (BARV) in the Falklands, and finally, AVREs were used in the Gulf War of 1990 to 1991.

The Final Wartime Developments
As we have seen, the war in the east had given the German *Panzerwaffe* (tank arm) some nasty shocks, particularly when they encountered the T-34—so much so that General Guderian, as inspector of armor, had suggested that the German armament industry simply copy the design. In 1944–45 the Germans had new shocks when they came up against most powerfully armed tank in World War II—the Tyazholy Tank IS Heavy Tank Iosef Stalin. The IS-2's improved fire control meant that it was almost a match for German Tigers and Panthers. The long 122mm M1943 gun, with its distinctive overhang, was an extremely powerful weapon. However, it fired two-part ammunition and so only 28 rounds could be carried and rates of fire were slow. During World War II tanks mainly used one-part "fixed" ammunition. Soviet tank commanders used the 12.7mm DshK1938 turret mounted heavy AA machine gun with its optical sight to engage German positions.

The IS-2 was used in action for the first time in February 1944 at Korsun Shevcherkov. The IS-2

INSET: *Although numerically the Sherman was the most important tank in British service, Britain's tank factories continued to produce large numbers of indigenous designs that generally lagged behind those of Germany and the Soviet Union. The standard British tank at the time of the Normandy campaign was the Cruiser Tank Mark VIII Cromwell.*

RIGHT: *With a frying pan attached to the last tank's hull rear, a line of Cromwells advances into action during the massive British and Canadian armored offensive known as Operation "Goodwood." Although fast and reliable, the Cromwell's armor was no match for the well dug-in 88s and Panzers and they suffered heavy losses.*

BELOW: *A line of German POWs passes a column of Shermans of the 4th Canadian Armoured Brigade as they advance from Caen to close the Falaise Gap, causing the cataclysmic defeat of the German armies in Normandy. These are M4A4 models or Sherman Vs in British and Canadian service, while the third tank from the left is a Firefly with the end of its long barrel disguised to deceive German antitank gunners who would otherwise target it first. Photograph dated August 8, 1944.*

INSET, RIGHT: *A Sherman VC Firefly advances through the village of Cantaloup on July 31, 1944. The Firefly was a highly successful project to upgun the Sherman with a 17pdr of greatly improved armor-piercing capability. The 17pdr can often be recognized by the prominent muzzle brake at the end of the barrel.*

After the close-quarter fighting during the Normandy campaign, the breakout into France allowed the M8 light armored cars of the reconnaissance units to sweep forward covering long distances in the pursuit of the retreating German forces. On August 25, 1944, Paris was liberated and here a group of M8 armored cars take part in the victory parade beneath the Arc de Triomphe.

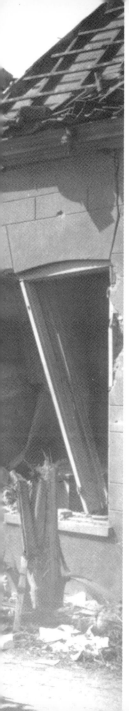

FAR LEFT: *Due to their superior firepower Sherman Fireflies were a priority target for German antitank gunners and tank crews. Various attempts were made to disguise the length of the 17pdr gun as on this Sherman Firefly IC Hybrid. It has a fake muzzlebrake half way down the barrel and the forward underside painted in a wavy pattern. Often using two colors, with another darker color along the top, this technique originated in Italy where the harsher light made the camouflage more effective but it was also used extensively in Northwest Europe during 1944.*

LEFT: *After years of brutal Nazi occupation, Belgian civilians cluster round the AFVs of their liberators including an M4A1 Sherman and M8 light armored car in the background. In the foreground stands an M10 3-inch gun motor carriage (GMC). Note the ammunition stowage inside the open turret and how vulnerable the interior is to artillery airburst shells.*

ABOVE: *Troops of the 39th Infantry Regiment, 9th Infantry Division, catch a lift on an M4A3 fitted with an M1 dozer blade of the 3rd Armored Division as it crosses the Siegfried Line through dragon teeth antitank obstacles on September 15, 1944.*

LEFT: *A Sherman M4A3 (76mm) crosses a pontoon bridge over the River Roer with the enhanced M1A1C 76mm gun in its T23 turret, and extended track grousers to give better floatation over soft ground. Despite these improvements, the Sherman remained inferior to the German Panthers and Tigers but its availability in vast numbers tipped the balance.*

had armor ranging from one to six inches thick, and though this restricted speed to 23mph it made it almost invulnerable. At the close of the war the Kirov factory produced the superb IS-3 with its distinctive sloped "frying pan" turret.

Like the Germans, the Russians made great use of assault guns. The best were ISU-152 and ISU-122. The ISU-152 weighed around 45 tons and had armor ranging from 1in to 3.5in thick. The ISU-152K, with external stowage and engine improvements, remained in production until 1952. The ISU-122 assault gun had a crew of five and the same gun as that fitted to the IS-2 tank. The ISU-152 and ISU-122 assault guns were grouped in independent heavy assault gun regiments and brigades.

The Tiger II

The last tank to be produced by the Germans as a counter to these formidable Soviet types was the Tiger II Ausf B, a powerful and well designed vehicle that combined the firepower of the

Tiger I with the design of the Panther. With a crew of five it was armed with one 8.8cm gun L/71; two 7.92mm MGs and had armor protection from 1.5in to 7in. Its chief drawback was its weight to power ration. It weighed just over 68 tons but its Maybach V-12 700bhp petrol engine gave atop speed of only 21mph and a range of around 100 miles.

The Tiger II was developed too late to have an effect on the war. In the end, for all the vaunted superiority of its vehicles, it was the power of Allied industry that counted. We have already discussed the position in Normandy—a potential Allied force of 5,300 tanks against 1,500 German tanks. On the Eastern Front the story was the same. In the fighting in July and August 1944 in Poland the USSR committed 6,000 tanks and AFVs against the German force of 1,800 and in January 1945 in the drive on the Oder they had 4,100 tanks to pit against the Germans 1,150. It is hardly surprising that the post-World War II world would see armor— and methods of destroying it—as the most significant issue on the land battlefield.

INSET: *Known as the Tiger II or King Tiger, the PzKpfw. VI Ausf. B (SdKfz. 182) was the most powerful German tank to see service during World War II, but fortunately for the Allies only 489 were built from January 1944 to March 1945 with much production being disrupted by allied strategic bombing. Nevertheless, with its more powerful 88mm main armament and well-sloped thick armor, it posed a formidable threat to allied tank crews although its mobility at 68 tons was suspect*

RIGHT: *The M10 3-inch GMC soon proved inadequate against the heavier German tanks and it was superseded by the M36 GMC armed with the more powerful M3 90mm gun as fitted to the M26 Pershing heavy tank. However, the M36 GMC was never available in sufficient numbers to replace the M10 GMC entirely, and the latter continued in service to the war's end with an improved high-velocity armor-piercing round that was capable of defeating most German AFVs.*

FAR RIGHT: *The Battle of the Bulge in December 1944 and January 1945 saw some of the most bitter fighting of the war on the Western Front in the most atrocious weather conditions as Hitler made one last gamble to defeat the Western alliance. American armored units were at a distinct disadvantage as only 25 percent were equipped with the more powerful 76mm-armed models.*

OPPOSITE, ABOVE: *Although outclassed by contemporary German designs, the M4 medium tank had several distinct virtues. It was simple to operate and mechanically reliable, but above all it was available in vast numbers. 49,234 Shermans were produced in the U.S. with a further 2,137 in Canada to give a grand total of 51,371. This is more than the combined total of all the tanks manufactured by Britain and Germany through-out World War II. In 1940, America had a tank production capacity measured in dozens while at the height of produc-tion, one Sherman was com-pleted every 24 minutes. This M4A3 shows several features of mid-production models with a front hull made from a one-piece casting, and the wider M34A1 gun mount. Combat experience soon showed that the Sherman was inadequately armored and extra plates were welded at vulnerable places such as along the hull sides where the ammunition was stowed.*

OPPOSITE, BELOW: *Indicative of the terrible conditions endured throughout the Battle of the Bulge, a group of M4A3 Shermans of the 40th Tank Battalion, 7th Armored Division wait to go into action near St. Vith on January 24, 1945, in the Ardennes region of Belgium.*

LEFT: *The M16 multiple gun motor carriage was an antiaircraft variant based on the M3 half-track. It was armed with quadruple .50cal machine guns. This M16 is shown on March 11, 1945, guarding the Remagen bridges across the Rhine with spare ammunition magazines on the ground and another M16 moving into position behind. Because of the lack of Luftwaffe aircraft as targets, such vehicles were often used as fire support in the ground role.*

There were scores of special purpose variants based on the basic M4 medium tank. One of the most spectacular was the Sherman Calliope, so named after the steam-powered musical organs at showgrounds. The T34 rocket launcher was mounted above the tank with its elevation and azimuth for firing controlled by the rotation of the turret with the elevating mechanism attached to the main gun. The rocket launcher weighed 1,840lb and comprised 60 4.5in fin-stabilized rockets in 90in long plastic tubes. If the tactical situation demanded, the complete assembly could be jettisoned and the vehicle reverted to being a standard gun tank. Both the Soviets and the Germans made wide use of free-flight rocket artillery such as the Katyusha and the Nebelwerfer but this was not the case with the western allies and the Calliope was one of the few tank mounted versions. Its purpose was to provide a high density of fire ahead of assault troops but they were never available in sufficient quantities to make this a reality when conventional tube artillery fulfilled the same role.

RIGHT: *The main gun of an M4A3 (76) HVSS Sherman provides covering fire to attacking infantry during the last desperate battles of World War II. This was the final model of the Sherman to be built during the war in a gradual process of evolution that ended with a much improved tank with no dramatic disruption of the mass-production process. Note that the allied white star on the turret has been subdued to remove a convenient aiming point for German antitank gunners.*

LEFT: *Once the western allies had broken the Atlantic Wall and were firmly lodged inside Hitler's Festung Europa following the D-Day landings, the defeat of the Nazis was assured with Germany trapped in a massive pincer as T-34s and IS tanks swept in from the east and M4 Shermans from the west supported by all the other types of AFVs that comprised a modern mechanized army. Here, in the closing weeks of the war the weapons forged in the arsenal of democracy advance into the ruins of Hitler's 1,000 Year Reich. The country that inflicted Blitzkrieg on the world had it visited upon it with crushing finality. Here, antitank mines are prepared; behind, in rough winter camouflage, an M18 GMC.*

An M7 105mm howitzer motor carriage motors past elements of the 314th Infantry Regiment, 79th Infantry Division. The M7 HMC was one of the most important variants of the M4 medium tank as it provided a self-propelled weapons' platform for the field artillery. It first saw action at the second Battle of El Alamein with the Eighth Army and in British service it was named the "Priest" because of the pulpit configuration for the .50cal machine gun.

FAR LEFT: *The M24 Chaffee was the final American light tank of World War II and 4,731 were built by August 1945. The first unit to be equipped with the M24 was the 744th Tank Battalion in January 1945 and it entered combat in the following month during Operation "Grenade"—the assault over the River Roer. These tank crews are undertaking tank gunnery practice near Eschweiler in Germany on February 12, 1945.*

BOTTOM LEFT: *An M7 105mm HMC crosses a pontoon bridge over a river in Germany. The M7 was a simple and robust weapon. Its main drawback was the lack of overhead protection—common to virtually all self-propelled guns in World War II.*

ABOVE LEFT: *The recovery of bogged and battle-damaged AFVs is an unglamorous and often overlooked skill but it is essential to maintain the mobility and the force numbers of any armored formation. Here a pair of M32 series tank recovery vehicles, based on the M4 Sherman chassis, winch a stranded companion from the 43rd Tank Battalion, 12th Armored Division, out of muddy terrain.*

LEFT: *The M18 Hellcat was the only purpose-designed tank destroyer that saw service with the U.S. Army. Although much smaller and faster than its M10 3in GMC contemporary, the Hellcat had superior firepower and 1,850 were built. They equipped 21 tank destroyer battalions in Europe and three in the Pacific campaign. However, the M18 had the same firepower as the 76mm armed Sherman and its high road speed of 60mph was of no consequence in the tank-destroyer role when its main armament was incapable of destroying a Panther at normal combat ranges except from the rear quarters.*

OPPOSITE: *With the crew's bedding rolls strapped to the back, an M3A1 half-track advances through the German village of Geiselhardt. The racks along the hull sides were designed to carry antitank mines but most crews preferred to carry ammo for their crew-served MGs.*

LEFT: *As the allies advanced into Germany so the number Panzerfaust and Panzerschreck hollow-charge antitank attacks grew. The relatively thin armor and poor internal stowage of ammunition and fuel of the M4 medium led to many catastrophic fires when a Sherman was penetrated. Numerous improvised methods were tried to thwart these weapons including racks of sandbags around the hull and turret.*

LEFT: *When the M4 medium was upgunned with the M1A1 76mm, the opportunity was taken to provide a safer ammunition stowage system with the main armament rounds now stowed in water jackets that much reduced the risk of fire if the tank was penetrated. Even so, the armor piercing capacity of the 76mm was not dramatically greater than the 75mm until the introduction of the HVAP or High Velocity Armor Piercing round. Until then the M4 Sherman was virtually incapable of penetrating the frontal armor of a PzKpfw. V Panther at any range whereas the latter could destroy a Sherman at all normal combat ranges; indeed, in one instance a 75mm round from a Panther passed through the front of a Sherman and its transmission housing, through the hull floor ammunition rack and then through the engine compartment and out of the rear hull. This Seventh Army vehicle passes burning buildings south of Frankfurt.*

RIGHT: *In time almost a third of US Army M4 Shermans in the European Theater of Operations were armed with the M1 76mm gun but the remainder retained the old 75mm to the end—such as these elderly M4A1 models with their characteristic cast hulls. In fact, the 75mm HE or high explosive round was superior to that of the 76mm with a charge of 1.47lb of explosive as against 0.86lb. As the war came to the closing stages there were far fewer tank vs tank clashes but numerous targets for HE so the older 75mm-equipped Shermans were valuable to the end. The early M4 and M4A1 models were powered by a Whirlwind radial gasoline engine that provided adequate horsepower but they were prone to catching fire when hit; so much so that U.S. tank crews nicknamed them "Ronsons" after the cigarette lighter. Nevertheless, the M4 was one of the outstanding AFVs of World War II and its contribution to allied victory was incalculable.*

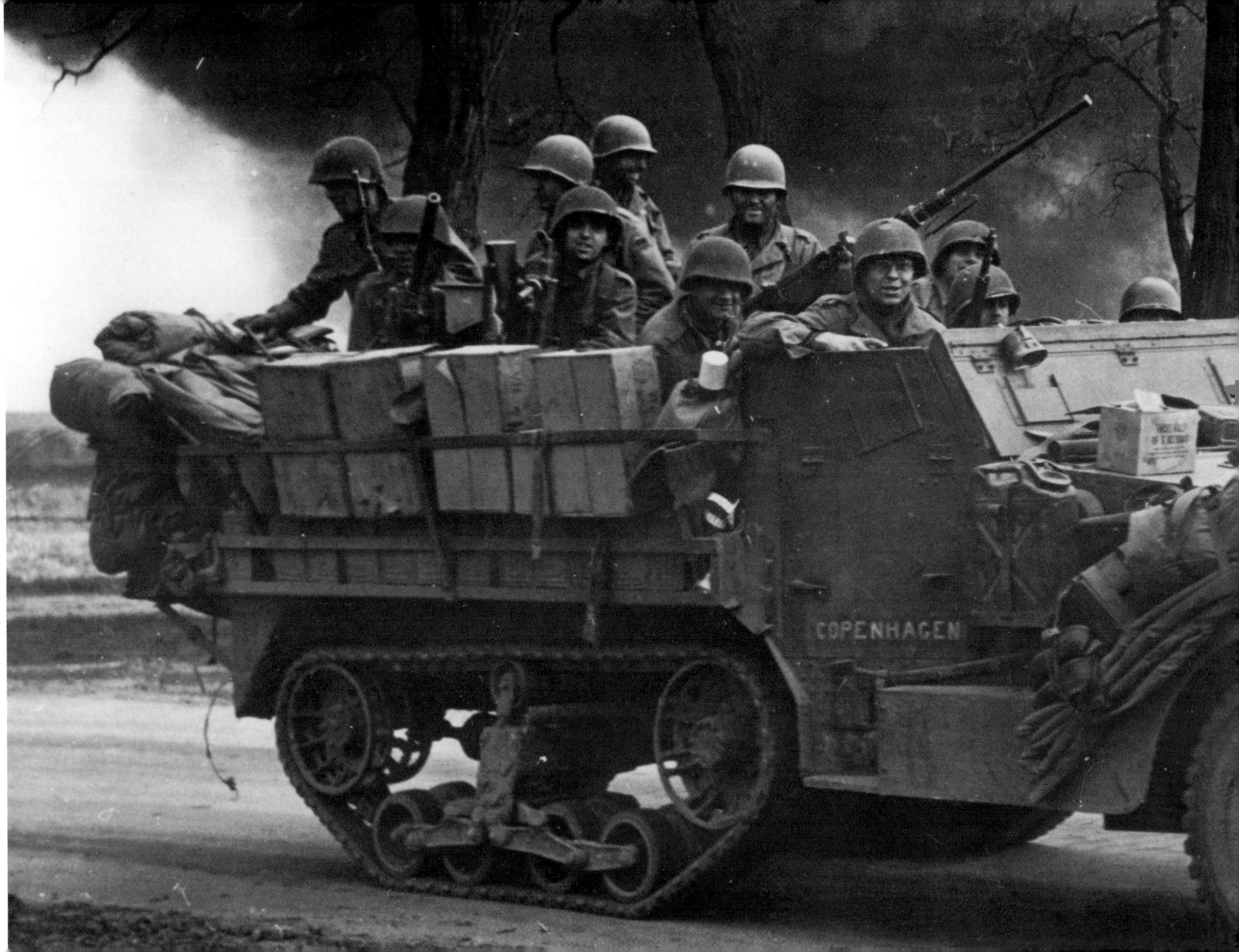
COPENHAGEN

ABOVE: *Two German PoWs help a wounded GI to an aid station in November 1944, passing an M4. The M4 medium came in four basic models. The original design was the M4 with a welded hull and Continental gasoline engine of which 8,389 were built. The M4A1 was built to the same specification as the M4 but with a cast hull and was the first model to be put into production with a total of 9,677 being built. The M4A2 was similar to the basic M4 but incorporated twin GM diesel truck engines; 11,283 were manufactured with most being supplied under Lend-Lease to the British and Soviets. This model was also used by the U.S. Marine Corps. The M4A3 was the standard medium tank of the U.S. Army. The M4A4 featured a lengthened hull to incorporate a Chrysler Multibank configuration of five six-cylinder engines powering a common drive shaft. 7,499 were built, and this was the main type supplied to the British. There were also hundreds of derivative models, modifications, and specialized vehicles based on the basic Sherman M4 chassis*

LEFT: *As the war progressed so new stowage racks were designed and fitted for the M3 half-track such as* Copenhagen *here of the 46th Armored Infantry, 5th Armored Division, near Wittenmoor in Germany on April 12, 1945. This M3 is festooned with equipment while the winch at the front*

OPPOSITE, ABOVE: *During World War II, Germany devised numerous weird and wonderful weapons that diverted essential resources from proven systems. These miniature AFVs are Goliath tracked demolition charges. Each vehicle contains 220lb of explosives and almost a mile of three-core cable with two to control its steering and the other to detonate the charge remotely once it had arrived at its objective—be it a pillbox or a minefield.*

OPPOSITE, BELOW: *An M4 medium tank lies abandoned after being rent asunder by a massive internal explosion after striking an anti-tank mine. The Sherman was very prone to catching fire, particularly the gasoline-powered models used by the British Army, when penetrated by enemy direct fire weapons. Indeed, the German tank crews' nickname for the Sherman was the "Tommy cooker."*

LEFT: *U.S. troops shelter behind an M8 light armored car. 8,640 M8s were made between March 1943 and June 1945 and it was employed in every theater of war. The crew of this M8 have removed the rear side skirts to prevent the build up of mud and have fitted snow chains to enhance mobility in icy conditions. The M8 was used by several armies during World War II including the British and Canadians, who named it the Greyhound; the Free French; the Poles; and it was also employed in the reconnaissance troop of the Brazilian 1st infantry Expeditionary Division in Italy.*

ABOVE: The Eastern Front was the scene of titanic armored battles unsurpassed in the annals of mechanized warfare. After the disastrous losses of 1941 and 1942, the Red Army created powerful armored formations that battered the German Army from the banks of the Volga to Berlin. The SU-76 was the successful combination of the obsolescent chassis of the T70 light tank and the Model 1942 76.2mm antitank gun. Originally conceived as a tank destroyer, it was subsequently used as a self-propelled artillery weapon once its antitank capability diminished against the newer generation of German tanks. By the end of the Great Patriotic War—as the Russians called World War II—over 12,500 SU-76 self-propelled guns had been built.

RIGHT: Following the example of the German Sturmgeschütz assault guns, the Soviets were quick to develop similar AFVs based on the ubiquitous T-34. With the appearance of the Tiger and Panther the standard T-34/76 gun tank was outclassed so a larger 85mm gun with limited traverse was mounted in an armored housing on a T-34 chassis as the SU-85. When the T-34/85 was introduced, the tank destroy-er version was improved by mounting a 100mm weapon to counter the new German heavy tanks such as the King tiger. In this role the SU-85 and SU-100 became known as the "Animal Killers" as their task was to engage and destroy the formidable Panthers and Tigers.

OPPOSITE, ABOVE: Named after the Soviet communist leader Joseph Stalin, the IS series of heavy tanks evolved from the earlier KV or Klimenti Voroshilov type that was slow and cumbersome and mounted the same main gun as the T-34/76. The first IS-1 was built in January 1944 with the definitive IS-2 in the following month. The IS-2 first saw combat with the 11th Separate Guards Heavy Tank Regiment in April against Tiger I tanks of the sPzAbt 503 (schwere Panzer Abteilung or heavy tank unit). IS heavy tanks were usually employed as the breakthrough element in a major offensive while the "Animal Killer" tank destroyer units engaged German AFVs. This IS-2 formation is rolling across the snow-covered terrain of East Prussia on January 31, 1945.

OPPOSITE, BELOW: The Red Army was supplied with thousands of tanks by the western allies but few of them found favor with Soviet troops. More important to the Soviet war effort were the tens of thousands of 2½-ton trucks that supported the armored and mechanized formations. This early production M3 light tank is supporting an attack by M3 Lee tanks in the background against German positions northeast of Stalingrad. The tank is named Suvorov along the hull side after the famous Russian general of the Napoleonic wars. Western tanks were not appreciated by Soviet crews because of their comparatively weak armor and poor guns; indeed the M3 Lee was known as "the grave for seven brothers."

ABOVE: *Thanks to its broad tracks and powerful 500hp diesel engine, the T-34 had excellent cross-country mobility, particularly in snowy and muddy conditions that characterized much of the year on the Eastern Front. This gave it a great tactical advantage over the earlier Panzers with their narrow tracks and high ground pressure. Soviet troops were adept at attacking under the most adverse weather conditions that often surprised the enemy. These T-34/76 Model 1943 tanks are mounting an attack in the Carpathian Mountains in April 1944.*

LEFT: *T-34/85 tanks of General Pavel Rotmistrov's 5th Guards Tank Army, part of Marshal Konstantin Rokossovsky's Second Belorussian Front, plunge through the forests of East Prussia during the massive Vistula-Oder offensive of January 1945 that took the Red Army into the heart of Nazi Germany.*

FAR LEFT: *Soviet infantrymen crouch behind the turret of a T-34 Model 1943 against enemy small-arms fire as a column of T34s advances into the city of Berlin in April 1945. The Model 43 was the final version of the T-34/76 and featured a hexagonal turret and a commander's cupola for better all-round vision—a serious problem in earlier models. Production of the T-34/76 ended in 1944 but they continued in service until well after the end of the war.*

LEFT: *The huge attrition rate on the Eastern Front saw the destruction of thousands of tanks. The life expectancy of a typical T-34 was measured in days and they littered the battlefield like this T-34/85 that has been reduced to the status of a German army unit signpost.*

RIGHT: *The Soviets were quick to appreciate the value and cost-effectiveness of heavy assault guns based on the chassis of redundant tanks. Originally based on the KV-1S, the ISU-122 mounted a powerful 122mm main armament while the ISU-152 shown here carried a 152mm howitzer. Designed in just 25 days, the ISU-152 was rushed into production in February 1943 to counter the emergence of the Tiger I. The ISU-152 was employed as a heavy assault gun in the offensive and in the anti-tank role when it acquired the name of "Zvierboi" or "animal hunter" in its task to destroy German Tiger and Panther tanks. These vehicles are from the 374th Guards Heavy Self-Propelled Artillery Regiment, 4th Tank Army, of Marshal Ivan Konev's First Ukranian Front, during the assault on the Polish city of Lvov which fell on July 27, 1944 during the height of the titanic Soviet offensive "Bagration" that wrought the destruction of the German Army Group Center and the Red Army at the gates of Warsaw.*

FAR RIGHT: *Soviet tanks commonly carried a three-digit tactical marking but the white stripes on this T-34/85 were added in spring 1945 during the advance to Berlin along with a white cross on the roof to act as a mutual recognition device to reduce the incidence of "friendly fire" from Anglo-American ground-attack aircraft.*

RIGHT: *The T-34 was arguably the most decisive tank of World War II, embracing the best of foreign ideas into a rugged and effective tank that was improved significantly with the introduction of the T-34/85 model in 1944. It continued to serve with armies across the world well into the 1980s.* Philip Royal

TOP: *A Sturmgeschütz III Ausf. G SdKfz. 142/1 complete with Schürzen supplementary armor negotiates a partially leveled anti-tank ditch during the titanic Battle of Kursk in July 1943—the largest tank battle in history. There were 28 independent Sturmgeschütz (StuG) detachments, four divisional StuG detachments, two 2nd Funklenk companies, and 12 StuG platoons with Luftwaffe field divisions on the Eastern Front at this time, and the StuG became increasingly important in the defensive battles that followed.*

ABOVE: *The Tiger I was heavily engaged in the Battle of Kursk such as this one of the schwere Panzer Kompanie/SS Panzer Regiment 2 of the "Das Reich" 2nd SS Panzer Grenadier Division. The unit insignia of a gnome is painted on the turret side forward of the tactical number S11 that indicates the first tank of 1st Platoon. This is a very early production model fitted with antipersonnel mine-throwers on the hull top and the twin apertures for the driver's periscope in the front plate above the vision visor.*

LEFT Comprehensive and secure radio communications are fundamental for the successful prosecution of mechanized warfare. The Germans excelled until their Enigma code was broken. After their occupation of much of Europe, the Germans pressed into service all manner of vehicles such as this French Citroen radio truck.

RIGHT: The weather conditions on the Eastern Front came as an awful shock to the German Army as it approached Moscow, particularly when the fall rains came in what the Russians call Rasputitsa or "the time without roads." Once the bitter winter came and the ground froze, mobility was restored but by then it was too late and Moscow was held. The German Army was ill-prepared for the depths of a Russian winter and thousands perished in an appalling frozen nightmare. During the winter of 1942–43, the Germans were better equipped to operate in the cold such as this Pzkpfw III Ausf. L of the Leibstandarte Adolf Hitler, the 1st SS-Panzer Grenadier Division, and its crew in their well-padded winter uniforms.

During World War II, mechanized warfare embraced a whole host of machines and AFVs from the humble dispatch rider on a motor bicycle to a 56-ton Tiger heavy tank. The Germans were the undisputed masters of armored warfare although their forces were never as mechanized as their western foes or even the Soviets in the later stages of the war. Although they had implemented the concept of Blitzkrieg, there were never sufficient APCs or support vehicles for a truly integrated Panzerwaffe. As a case in point, of the 226 mechanized infantry battalions in September 1942, only 26 were actually mounted in SdKfz. 251 half track APCs.

RIGHT: *The T-34/85 first saw combat in late March 1944 during the Battle for the Hube Pocket on the Ukrainian/Romanian border, but in very limited numbers. Nevertheless, it was received enthusiastically by the troops of First Tank Army as it gave them a tank that almost matched the capabilities of the Panther and was markedly superior to the most common German tank of the period, the PzKpfw. IV Ausf. H and J. There were just 304 Panthers at the Eastern Front by the end of May 1944 by when the T-34/85 was being produced at the rate of over 1,000 a month. This Sixth Tank Army T-34/85 Model 1944 with perforated steel road wheels provides a fine comparison with the T-34/76 in the background.*

LEFT: *A T-34 Model 1943 and supporting infantry approach a burning PzKpfw. IV Ausf. G. The T-34 if fitted with a supplementary 40-liter fuel container on the hull rear to extend its range in the far reaches of the Eastern Front. Subsequently, three cylindrical drums were mounted on the hull sides with two on the left hand side and one on the right.*

BELOW LEFT: *Soviet Cossacks, supported by Russian-manned, British-made Valentine medium tanks, launch an attack against a German defensive position in late 1943. In the opening battles of Operation "Barbarossa" from June 1941, the Red Army lost thousands of tanks, although most of them were obsolescent types such as T-28 Medium Tank and T-26 Light Tank, in an attack accompanied by horsed cavalry. In one such encounter with German Panzers, a Soviet cavalry formation lost 2,000 men without a single German casualty. Fortunately, for the Red Army, the tanks that replaced the T-26 and T-28 types were far more potent and included the famed T-34 and KV-1.*

BELOW: *A Sturmgeschütz III Ausf. G moves forward in support of Waffen-SS troops during Operation "Citadel" against the Kursk salient in July 1943. Generally recognized as the largest armored clash in history, the battle of Kursk involved a German force of 196 Panthers, 181 Tigers, 597 PzKpfw. IIIs, and 615 PzKpfw. IVs as well as 520 assault guns pitted against 3,444 Soviet tanks with hundreds more held in reserve. Kursk was the death ride of the Panzerwaffe and thereafter the Germans were on the defensive strategically for the rest of the war.*

THIS PAGE: *German tank production during World War II lagged behind the Allies. Between 1939 and 1944 Germany built only 25,000 tanks: compare this to the Allied figures of : Britain 28,000; United States 76,000; USSR over 80,000. The first German assault guns, the Sturmgeschütz IIIs, (above and above left) appeared in 1940 and over 10,000 had been produced by the end of the War.*

LEFT, FARLEFT AND RIGHT: *Although the Panther and Tiger have captured the public imagination as the great tanks of the German armored forces of World War II, it was the PzKpfw. IV that was the backbone of the Panzerwaffe throughout the war. Originally armed with short 75mm gun designed for infantry support, it was progressively upgunned and uparmored as the opposing threats increased. This is the PzKpfw. IV Ausf. F2 that introduced the longer and more powerful 75mm KwK40 L/43 main gun to meet the challenge of the T34 and KV1 on the Eastern Front. This particular tank belonged to the elite Wehrmacht Grossdeutschland Division as part of the Fourth Panzer Army during the attack on Voronezh in July 1942.*

RIGHT: *Like the Sherman, the T-34 was produced in vast numbers that overcame most of its deficiencies. These included a cramped two-man turret with the commander also acting as gunner whereby neither duty was fulfilled properly. Furthermore, his vision from under armor was far worse than German tanks, which gave them a distinct tactical advantage in any battle. Beside the commander, the crew comprised a loader, driver, and a hull machine gunner who also manned the radio, if one was fitted, but most early T-34 did not have one. This made tactical control of any tank unit in battle an inexact science.*

BELOW: *A Soviet officer briefs his tank commanders during the harsh winter warfare on the Eastern Front with the snow-camouflaged tanks standing ready in the background. These are early production versions of the T-34 Model 1943 with twin crew hatches in the turret roof instead of the cumbersome and heavy single type of earlier models. The T-34 came as a rude shock to the Germans as it rendered most of their tank and antitank guns obsolete.*

FAR RIGHT: *By the lights of 1941, the T-34 was an outstanding tank that combined the three essential attributes of firepower, mobility, and armor protection to a high degree. It was also simple to operate and, once the tank factories had been moved eastward behind the protection of the Ural mountains, produced in overwhelming numbers. It was only the superior training and tactical awareness of Panzer crews that allowed the Germans to succeed in 1941 and 1942. The T-34 was one of the great tanks of World War II, and it remains an icon of the Great Patriotic War to this day. Due to a lack of infantry carriers, Soviet troops rode into battle on the backs of the tanks—a tactic that was known as "desant." For this purpose, the T-34 was provided with numerous handrails around the turret and along the hull sides. These T-34/76 Model 1943 tanks of the Third Guards Tank Army with their "desant" teams are taking part in Operation "Kutuzov," the Soviet counter-offensive on the Briansk Front following the battle of Kursk, on August 4, 1943, in the attack on Orel which was recaptured on the following day.*

ABOVE: *The hulls of redundant gun tanks were routinely converted by the Germans for other roles such as this 150mm Schwere Infanteriegeschütz 33 (Sf) auf Pzkpfw 38(t) —the last part of the designation indicating it was based on the former Czech TNHP or PzKpfw.. 38(t) chassis. The self-propelled howitzer was also known as the "Grille" or cricket and it served in Russia, Tunisia, Italy and France from early 1943 onward.*

LEFT: *The scale of the conflict on the Eastern Front was colossal and the casualties were commensurate. These PzKpfw. IV Ausf. H tanks of XXXXVIII Panzer Corps lie burning on the street of Kiev after its recapture by Soviet forces on November 6, 1943— just in time for the annual celebration of the Russian Revolution.*

LEFT: *By the summer of 1944, the Germans had lost the priceless military advantage of air superiority on both the Eastern and Western Fronts. From then on any movement by day was liable to be subjected to incessant attack from allied aircraft, and camouflage became a life-saving necessity, such as this Tiger I of the 3rd SS Panzer Division "Totenkopf" as protection against the "jabos" (fighter-bombers).*

Both the Germans and the Soviets made whatever use they could with captured enemy equipment such as this PzKpfw. III Ausf. J and a line of StuG. III assault guns appropriated by Russian troops during the battle for Moscow in the winter of 1941. Given a wash of winter camouflage, the leading vehicle is daubed in Cyrillic with the slogan— "Death to the Fascist Invaders."

These damaged PzKpfw. III tanks were being despatched for repair following the battle of Kursk when they were captured by the Soviets in August 1943. This view gives an interesting comparison between the 50mm KwK L/42 and the longer 50mm KwK39 L/60 and the supplementary armor fitted to the gun mantlet.

The PzKpfw. VI Ausf. E first saw combat on the Eastern Front with the 1.Kompanie/schwere Heeres Panzer Abteilung 502 on August 29, 1942, where it came as a severe shock to the Soviets as they had no knowledge of this powerful heavy tank that was known as the Tiger. The Tiger was deployed in schwere Panzer Abteilungen (heavy tank detachments) or as independent units that were attached to other formations for specific operations. There were 14 Tigers in each company and up to three companies in each detachment. Tiger companies were also issued to several SS divisions and as independent SS units of schwere SS Panzer Abteilungen. With only 1,354 produced between July 1942 and August 1944, the Tiger I was always in short supply and units were rarely if ever at full strength but their reputation on the battlefield was without equal and few tanks have inspired such fear in their enemies. As a case in point, from the start of the battle of Kursk on July 5, 1943, until September, the 503rd's H.Pz.Abt. destroyed 501 enemy tanks, 388 anti-tank guns, 79 artillery weapons, and seven aircraft at a cost of just 18 Tigers of which only seven were totally destroyed. The Tiger I remains one of the world's most legendary tanks of all in the history of mechanized warfare.

The scourge of the Swastika was crushed beneath the tracks of IS heavy tanks and T-34s in the final savage battles in the streets of Berlin in May 1945. An elderly wounded Volksturm looks on forlornly as a column of Soviet armor lines up before the Brandenburg Gate in the heart of Berlin after the city's capitulation.

LEFT: *Too late to see combat in World War II, the IS3 heavy tank and its formidable 122mm main armament came as a rude shock to the western powers when it appeared at the Allied victory parades to mark the end of the war. Britain and American had nothing to compare with this powerful tank and it presented an awful specter of Soviet dominance in tank design for several years, although the vehicle was dogged by mechanical problems for a long time. Known to its crews as the "Pike" from the shape of its nose, this IS-3 is taking part in the victory parade held in Kiev, one of only four 'Hero Cities' of the Soviet Union to be awarded such an accolade for its fortitude during the Great Patriotic War.*

PAGES 140-145: Contrary to popular perception, tanks and AFVs were used extensively in the Pacific war. Indeed, over a third of US armor battalions were deployed in the Hoe. The whole gamut of American AFVs was employed with the M3/M5 light tank series and the M4 family predominating. With its light weight and high mobility, the M3/M5 was well suited to negotiating the forbidding terrain and jungle trails of the Far East and Pacific islands although its 37mm main armament was often inadequate against Japanese bunker systems. Operating in pairs to provide mutual protection against fanatical infantry attack, a special canister round was developed akin to a giant buckshot cartridge to counter enemy troops at close quarter that came in ammunition crates marked "For Use Against Japanese Only." The 75mm M8 HMC (page 140 and opposite) was developed from the M5 chassis to add more firepower. In time the M4 Sherman (page 141, opposite, above left, left and far left) became the principal tank of choice with both U.S. Army and U.S. Marine Corps armor battalions. In any encounter with Japanese AFVs, U.S. tanks proved to be consistently superior from Tarawa to Okinawa. But of all the AFVs of the Pacific war the most notable was the LVT—Landing Vehicle Tracked. Commonly known as the Amtrac from its original designation of amphibian tractor, the LVT (top left) was fundamental to the U.S. victory in the Central Pacific. Designed by Donald Roebling in the 1930s as the Alligator for operating in the flooded Florida Everglades, over 10,000 LVTs were employed by the US Marine Corps for their primary role of assault from the sea:
"From the halls of Montezuma, to the shores of Tripoli,
We fight our country's battles in the air, on land and sea.
First to fight for right and freedom, and to keep our honor clean;
We are proud to claim the title of United States Marine."

THE POSTWAR YEARS

In the years that followed the defeat of Nazi Germany in 1945, NATO squared up in Europe opposite the Warsaw Pact. In the light of their experience of invasion in 1941, the leadership of the USSR adopted an aggressive defense strategy that envisaged attacking the West. The USSR and its Eastern European allies with the Warsaw Pact were equipped with some well-designed and versatile armored vehicles. East would face West in combat, but only in small "proxy" wars as the two superpowers jockeyed for influence around the world.

The T-54 series tanks first appeared in 1949 as replacements for the T-34 tank of World War II. The first T-54 prototype was completed in 1946 with first production beginning in 1947. The T-54 was continuously improved and modified, and when sufficient changes had been made, the tank was redesignated T-55. The T-55 was introduced in 1958 and incorporated all the refinements and improvements of the fully developed T-54 series without being radically different in design or appearance. The T-55A appeared in the early 1960s. The T-54/55 tanks have been produced in greater quantity than any other tank in the world. Seven main production models have been widely used throughout the Warsaw Pact and in many other countries. The T-54/55 series has been manufactured in Czechoslovakia and Poland as well as in China where it is known as Type 59.

The T-55 combined a high-velocity gun with a highly mobile chassis, a low silhouette, and exceptional long-range endurance. Improvements over the T-54 include a larger V-12 water-cooled diesel engine with 580hp rather than 520hp, increased cruising range of 500km (up to 715km with two 200-liter auxiliary fuel tanks that could be carried mounted on the rear deck) rather than 400km (600km with auxiliary tanks). The T-55 also has two-plane stabilization of the main gun rather than vertical stabilization only, and a basic load for

LEFT: *Following the North Korean invasion on June 25, 1950, tanks were quickly despatched to South Korea to bolster the U.S. troops trying to stem the communist onslaught. However, the only tanks immediately available were M24 Chaffee light tanks and M4A3 (76) HVSS Sherman models that were hard pressed to counter the T-34/85 tanks of the North Korean 105th Armored Brigade.*

INSET: *At the outset of the Korean War, the principal tanks of the U.S. Army were the World War II-vintage M26 Pershing and an improved version of the latter fitted with a diesel engine and designated M46 Patton. At the same time a new medium tank known as the M47 was in production but it did not serve in Korea.*

FAR LEFT: *The M4 Sherman continued in service for several years with the U.S. Army following World War II with early models such as this M4A1 serving as training vehicles. These Shermans are conducting an amphibious warfare exercise from an LST in 1947.*

LEFT: Among the first effective tanks to arrive in Korea were the M26 medium tanks of the U.S. Marine Corps that arrived in time to secure the Pusan Pocket around the last surviving major port of South Korea.

TOP: Tanks equipped with flamethrowers had proved fearsomely effective against entrenched diehard Japanese troops during the Pacific campaign. A number were shipped to Korea to reinforce the tank battalions such as this M4A3 (76) HVSS with a flamethrower in place of the hull machine gun.

ABOVE: The first encounter between Marine M26 Pershings and communist tanks occurred on August 17, 1950, when T-34/85s of the 105th Armored Brigade attacked the "Naktong Bulge" of the Pusan perimeter. Used to fighting the ineffective M24 Chaffee and demoralized South Korean infantry, the T-34s advanced unsupported to fall prey to the 90mm guns of the M26s of the 1st Marine Provisional Brigade.

RIGHT: *The M19 GMC was based on the chassis of the M24 light tank. It mounted twin 40mm Bofors guns in a rear-mounted turret as a self-propelled anti-aircraft weapon, but as there was no real air threat in Korea these AFVs were used in the ground support role.*

BELOW RIGHT: *1951 was the Year of the Tiger in the Chinese astrological calendar and many U.S. tanks were painted the tiger heads, claws and stripes prior to the spring offensive to instil fear in the supposedly superstitious Chinese troops.*

FAR RIGHT: *The T-34/85 proved to be highly effective in the initial communist offensive as South Korean troops had few antitank weapons beyond simple bazookas. Approximately 250 T-34/85 tanks were committed and almost all were destroyed by the end of September with air-dropped napalm being a deadly antitank weapon.*

the main gun of 43 rounds rather than 34. The 100mm rifle-bore main gun had a bore evacuator at the muzzle. There were two 7.62mm machine guns, one coaxial one bow, the latter omitted in the later T-55A version.

Used in the invasion of Hungary in 1956, Czechoslovakia in 1968, and Syria in 1970, the T-55 was the main Arab tank in the 1967 and 1973 wars with Israel. During the 1970s, the T-54 saw combat in Vietnam, Cambodia, and Uganda. Type 59s were part of the Iraqi order of battle in the two Gulf wars. Large numbers are still in service, although by the 1980s the T-54/55 had been replaced by the T-62, T-64, T-72, and T-80 as the primary main battle tank in first-line Soviet tank and motorized rifle units. The latest tank in the Russian order of battle is the T-90 equipped with a 125mm gun capable of firing either shells or missiles.

The Soviet Union had a major surprise for NATO when in November 1967 at a Red Square parade, observers saw the *Bronevaya Maschina Piekhota* (BMP-1) for the first time, even though vehicles had been in production since the early 1960s. NATO designated it the M-1967 and BMP. The BMP represented an important shift from the concept of an armored personnel carrier (APC), or as some soldiers knew it, "a battle taxi," to an armored infantry combat vehicle (ICV), combining high mobility, effective anti-tank weapons, and armored protection for carrying troops.

The BMP was significantly smaller than Western APCs and had considerably greater fire-power. The BMP-1 was innovative in that it allowed the infantry inside to fire their personal weapons from within the vehicle while remaining protected by armor. To do this, firing ports and vision devices were provided for each infantry soldier. Thus the BMP became the first ICV. The BMP-1 carried a crew of three to eight and BMPs replaced the wheeled BTR-50Ps and complemented the BTR-60PBs in first-line motorized rifle regiments.

BELOW: *By the end of 1950, the United Nations' invasion of North Korea had been thwarted following the intervention of the Chinese armed forces. The front lines stabilized close to the original prewar border. By now numerous tank battalions were deployed to Korea and the fighting degenerated into positional warfare.*

LEFT: *U.S. Marines engage enemy forces in the hills with their .50cal machine guns mounted on the turrets of these M26 Pershings of Company C, 1st Marine Tank Battalion and an M4A3 105mm Howitzer tankdozer without its blade during an operation on March 15, 1951.*

OVERLEAF: *The primitive road system in Korea was hardly capable of supporting heavy armor. Tanks were largely confined to the unpaved tracks on the valley floors that weaved through the surrounding hills and mountains where the unmechanized communist forces sought cover from the superior firepower of U.N. troops.*

A combination of effective antitank firepower, high mobility, and adequate protection made the BMP a formidable addition to the inventory of Soviet motorized rifle regiments. Designed to suit the demands of high-speed offensive in a nuclear war, it carried a 73mm 2A20 gun with 40 rounds, and maximum range of over 2,500m. It could also fire a rocket-assisted, fin-stabilized, HEAT projectile with an effective range of 800m (capable of successfully engaging tanks at ranges up to 1,300m) and was equipped with an automatic loader. A launching rail for the AT-3 "Sagger" antitank guided missile was located above the gun for longer range antitank capability (up to 3,000m). The BMP infantry combat vehicle became the basis for a family of variants. Many BMPs now mount either the improved, semiautomatic AT-3c "Sagger" or the new AT-4 "Spigot" or AT-5 "Spandrel" ATGM.

The Arab-Israeli wars of 1967 and 1973 saw Soviet vehicles, equipment, and doctrine tested against their Western equivalents fielded by the Israelis. In 1967 a force of 1,000 Israeli tanks was faced by 1,300 Egyptian, 500 Syrian, and 250 Jordanian. Victory went to Israel in part because it achieved air superiority and also because it had well-trained and highly motivated tank crews. In October 1973 the numbers had increased; now 2,000 Israeli tanks were faced by 2,500 Egyptian, 1,500 Syrian, and available on call 200 Jordanian and 600 Iraqi tanks.

Because of the extreme vulnerability demonstrated by the BMP in the 1973 war, there was been extensive debate in the Soviet Army as to how it should be used in battle. The BMP had relatively thin armor (maximum thickness 19mm in the hull, 23mm in the turret) which provided protection against .50cal armor-piercing rounds only over the 60° frontal arc, and the vehicle was extremely vulnerable to ATGM and tank fire. Due to its compact design, critical areas such as the engine compartment and ammunition storage area (on the right side), fuel cells (in the rear doors), and the troop compartment were located in such a manner that penetration anywhere on the vehicle normally resulted in a mobility, firepower, or personnel kill.

Despite this the BMP and its variants was widely exported and has seen action in Africa as

ABOVE: *Tank-mounted searchlights were introduced in March 1952 to assist tank crews in engaging enemy troops at night when the communists often mounted attacks to nullify the superior firepower of U.N. air support.*

LEFT: *Troops of the 9th Infantry Division of the 2nd Infantry Division with attached Republic of Korea soldiers move out on the back of an M26 Pershing in a counterattack against communist forces near the Naktong river on September 3, 1950.*

Men of 1st Marine Tank Battalion replenish their M46 Patton with 90mm main armament ammunition between fire missions in November 1951. The tank is park on a slope to increase elevation in the fire-support role.

INSET: *The two most effective American tanks during the early months of the Korean War were the M26 Pershings of U.S. Marine tank battalions and the refurbished M4A3 (76mm) HVSS medium tanks that had been on occupation duties in Japan. The first U.S. tanks to clash with North Korean armor were M24 Chaffees that were outclassed by the heavier T-34/85s.*

LEFT: *During the period of positional warfare from mid-1951 onwards, tanks were employed as direct fire support weapons for the forward infantry units. This M46 Patton of the 1ST Marine Tank Battalion is flying a Turkish flag indicating it was operating in support of Turkish troops attached to the US 25th Infantry Division.*

well as the Middle East. It would be the basis of a family of tracked vehicles including the BMD-3 airborne combat vehicle, the BMP-2 and BMP-3.

As the Group of Soviet Forces in Germany were fielding the BMP, NATO's answer was the slab-sided M113. Like the Bell UH-1 "Huey" helicopter, the M113 APC became an icon of the Vietnam War, being seen throughout that conflict from before the arrival of American troops to after their eventual departure. The Israelis replaced their half-tracks with M113s following the 1967 war and the Australian and New Zealand armies adopted the vehicle.

The origins of the M113 date back to January 1956 when the Army Ordnance Tank-Automotive Command (ATAC) began a program to design and build a lightweight APC for armored and infantry units. The requirement called for amphibious and air-droppable capability and for high mobility over all types of terrain. The use of aluminum armor seemed to offer many advantages over steel, and the industrial basis for mass-production of the material was there as a by-product of the aircraft industry.

With a crew of 2 and 11 soldiers, the minimum armament for the M113A1 varied but the minimum was usually one 0.50in (12.7mm) MG. Maximum armor was 1.77in. Powered by a General Motors 6V53; 6-cylinder 212hp diesel, it had a top speed of 38mph on land; propelled by its tracks the 11.16-tons vehicle could travel at 3mph in water. Its range was 298 miles.

The biggest users outside the U.S. were Israel with over 6,000 and Italy with over 3,000, most of which were produced locally by Otobreda, who exported many examples. Almost every user has developed specialist versions and added their own modifications.

In March 1945 a new tank entered service with the U.S. Army and was type standardized as the M26 Heavy Tank. About 300 saw action in Northwest Europe and another batch saw combat at Okinawa in May. For the first time the U.S. named a tank—General Pershing after the hard-riding US officer General "Black Jack" Pershing.

At last the U.S. Army had a tank able to confront the Tiger and Panther on equal terms, although the M3 90mm gun proved to be

ABOVE: *An M46 Patton of the 6th Tank Battalion, 24th Infantry Division, acts as a mail delivery service to troops on the front lines near Kumsong on December 7, 1951.*

RIGHT: *Resplendent in the full Tiger scheme of teeth, claws, and stripes, an M46 of B Company, 6th Tank Battalion, 24th Infantry Division pulls a stranded companion out of a boggy paddyfield during an action at Munsan-Ni in March 1951.*

slightly inferior to the German "88s." Onboard ammunition stowage for the 90mm M3 gun was 70 rounds. Armor protection was equal to the Tiger, helped by careful sloping, and maneuverability was superior. The M26A1 had the longer 90mm T15 gun, some of which were equipped with stabilization in the vertical axis.

Although none were available in theater, when fighting broke out in 1950, Pershings were quickly rushed to Korea where they helped counter the advance of the North Korean and Chinese T-34/85 tanks that had defeated lighter opposition. The sloped armor, large road wheels, and torsion bar suspension led the way to post-World War II U.S. tank designs up to the M60 series. The Korean War saw a force of 240 North Korean tanks reduced to zero and the US force rise from 20 to about 1,000 by the close of the fighting.

The M48 Patton was rushed into production because of the Korean War and Berlin crisis, and like the M47 suffered from many initial faults, large numbers of vehicles having to be rebuilt soon after delivery. Nevertheless, the M48 matured into an effective and popular tank.

In Vietnam, where Marine Corps M48s first arrived in 1965, combat was often at such close quarters that the gunner was more useful on the back of the vehicle with a grenade launcher while the commander fired the main gun. Chain-link fence was often hung on the tank or erected beside it when stopped, as this would snag or detonate B40 antitank rockets at a safe distance. One of the most distinctive additions was a one-million-candlepower Xenon searchlight with white and infrared light modes. The M48A3 had the British-designed 105mm gun which was first tested on the M48A1E1. Most of the 1,019 U.S. examples were created by rebuilding A1s and A2s. Israel has modified its M48s so often and so much that most remaining examples have more in common with the M60. During the invasion of Lebanon in 1982 they were among the first tanks to be fitted with explosive reactive armor (ERA).

Although the M48 was the peak of development through several "interim" models beginning with the M26 in 1944, the U.S. Army soon sought to improve on it. Three M48A2s were re-engined with the Continental AVDS-1790 diesel

M4A3 (76mm) HVSS Shermans of the 17th Tank Company, 17th Regimental Combat Team of the 7th Infantry Division are replenished with ammunition prior to an attack on March 12, 1951.

in February 1958 and later that year fitted with the new M68 gun, derived from the British Centurion's L7A1 105mm which elevates from minus 10° to plus 20°. These XM60s were found satisfactory and the type was standardized as the M60 in March 1959. Later models of M48 would be rebuilt with the same gun and powerplant, making it difficult to distinguish them from M60s. The M68 carries 63 rounds of APFSDS, APDS, HESH, HEAT, and smoke ammunition.

The M60A3 was the main version, introduced into production in 1978. The main improvements were a thermal sight (TTS), a laser rangefinder, the RISE engine, and a Halon fire suppression system. About 1,600 M60A3s were new-build and the rest were converted from M60A1s of various standards for a total of over 5,400 delivered to U.S. forces. The M60 has seen action in Arab-Israeli conflicts, and U.S. Marine

Corps tanks fitted with ERA fought in the Gulf War of 1991. Foreign operators include or included Austria, Egypt, Greece, Italy, Jordan, Morocco, Portugal, Saudi Arabia, Spain, Taiwan, Thailand, and Turkey.

The U.S. Army no longer fields the M60. It has been replaced by the M1 Abrams with its 120mm smooth-bore gun. The Abrams saw action in the 1991 Gulf War and the invasion of Iraq. Since its opposition was either Type 59 or at best T-72 tanks with ill-trained crews, neither could be called a test of this modern AFV.

In the late 1960s the Scorpion 76mm was developed by Alvis in the UK as a replacement for the Saladin armored car the Scorpion was officially designated FV101 Combat Vehicle, Reconnaissance, Tracked or CVR(T). This rather cumbersome title masked the fact that it was a speedy three-man light tank armed with a 76mm

BELOW LEFT: *By September 1950 South Korea had been virtually over-run, but on September 15 General Douglas MacArthur conducted a masterly counterstroke with amphibious landings at Inchon close to the South Korean capital of Seoul. Spearheaded by U.S. Marine armor, the capital was liberated on September 27 after savage street fighting. Here, U.S. Marines and their M26 Pershing wait to board an LST for the Inchon landings.*

BELOW: *With a Tiger's head on the glacis plate, an M4A3 of the 7th Cavalry Regiment of 1st Cavalry Division moves north of Chipyong on February 27, 1951, during Operation "Killer," the major U.N. counteroffensive against Chinese forces.*

LEFT: *With the fiber cases of 90mm projectiles littering the ground, an M46 Patton of C Company, 6th Tank Battalion, fires in support of men of the 24th Infantry Division on January 10, 1952.*

BELOW: *An M4A3 HVSS POA-CWS-H5 of the 1st Marine Tank Battalion advances on the central Korean front in the Wonju-Hoensong area on February 23, 1951. This Sherman variant mounted a flamethrower beside the 105mm howitzer. The flamethrower had a range of 100yd and a capacity to fire approximately 80 one-second bursts of flame.*

gun lighter than that in the Saladin. The first prototype was completed in 1969 and the first production vehicles appeared in 1972. What marked these vehicles out was the powerplant—a Jaguar 4.2-liter petrol engine producing 190bhp at 4,750rpm and a speed of 50mph.

By 1999, well over 3,500 had been built for the British Army and for export. Iranian Scorpions saw action during the Iran-Iraq war and in 1982 British Scorpions proved very effective in the Falklands campaign.

The FV107 Scimitar is, in effect, the Scorpion chassis with a turret armed with a 30mm Rarden cannon. The first prototype was completed in July 1971. The British Army received the vehicle in March 1974, and the Belgian Army in April that year. It would see action in the 1991 Gulf War engaging Iraqi Type 59s with AP and HE ammunition.

Tanks, infantry combat vehicles, and specialized armor have come a very long way from the clumsy vehicles that lumbered forward across no man's land in World War I. However, they still embody the same concept of shock action and principles of firepower, protection, and mobility.

In the opening years of the 21st century tanks have taken on something of the character of combat aircraft. Many of the decision and command functions have been computerized, and systems undreamed of even 50 years ago—such as global positioning systems (GPS) and laser rangefinding—have "digitized the battlefield."

GPS embedded into radios will allow a commander to know exactly where his tanks are located, without having to ask the crew to transmit their grid reference. The radios will be frequency hopping and consequently impossible to intercept.

The laser rangefinder linked into a ballistic computer allows the gunner or commander to locate a target; thereafter, the selection of ammunition type, elevation and charge, and allowance for windage, range, and other ballistic factors are entirely automatic.

Automatic loaders remove the need for a human loader and consequently the size of the tank and its silhouette can be reduced.

Armor technology, including explosive reactive armor (ERA) and Chobham ceramic armor, has made the main battle tank invulnerable to all but the most sophisticated antitank weapons or massive overkill by laser-guided 250kg bombs.

It is perhaps ironic therefore, that as the tank has achieved what may be its development apogee, it may actually be becoming obsolete. The principles of firepower, mobility, and protection that have defined tank design have little relevance in a world dominated by "the war on terror."

Tanks are very blunt weapons in a war that is fought using intelligence both human and electronic, precision targeting, and conducted principally by infantry on the ground. Deploying tracked vehicles in towns and cities looks heavy handed and smacks of the Communist regimes of Eastern Europe it can be politically insensitive.

Armor will continue to have its place on the battlefield, but in a world freed from the terror of the Cold War these vehicles may be wheeled, airportable, and amphibious and therefore capable of deployment at short notice to remote and primitive trouble spots.

They will become the cavalry of the 21st century whose distant bugle call, albeit now in the form of a transmission bounced off a communications satellite, will be the signal that help is on its way.

RIGHT: *Infantrymen scramble for cover as mortar fire falls near an M4A3 (76mm) HVSS of the 32nd Regimental Combat Team of the 7th Infantry Division after it ran over an antitank mine on the outskirts of Hadaewa on February 28, 1951.*

FAR RIGHT: *A Marine M4A3 (105mm) howitzer tank uses its M1A1 dozer blade to extricate a Jeep mired in the mud during the spring thaw in February 1951.*

OPPOSITE, ABOVE AND BELOW LEFT: *Initially, armored fighting vehicles were thought to be inappropriate in the hostile terrain of South Vietnam with its numerous waterways and glutinous paddyfields, but in March 1962 a batch of 32 M113 APCs was deployed to Vietnam for trials with the Army of the Republic of Vietnam (ARVN) mechanized rifle companies. Being fully amphibious, the M113 was well suited to negotiating the many rivers and boggy terrain, and soon proved to be an indispensable weapon in the ARVN armory. The M113 first saw combat on June 11, 1962, and it fought throughout the war in all regions of the country.*

CENTER LEFT AND LEFT: *Each of the Air Defense Artillery battalions in Vietnam were reinforced by a battery of truck-mounted M55 .50cal machine guns. The M55 "Quads" were mounted on the back of the M35 and M54 series of trucks. With no air threat in Vietnam, they were employed in the fire-support role as convoy escorts or perimeter defense when their awesome firepower was a potent deterrent to enemy attacks. Supply convoys remained highly ` vulnerable to ambush throughout the war, therefore many trucks were fitted with armored bodies bristling with machine guns as a countermeasure.*

ABOVE: *AFVs were highly effective in the defense of base camps and fire-support bases that were dotted across Vietnam. The Vietcong and North Vietnamese Army (VC/NVA) often attacked bases at night but tank-mounted searchlights and main armament weapons firing a deadly combination of Beehive rounds and automatic weapons frequently broke such assaults and saved the position from being overrun.*

LEFT: *An M48A3 of the 3rd Platoon, Company A of the 1st Tank Battalion, supports Marines of 1/5th Marines during the savage street fighting in Hue City on February 12, 1968, during the VC/NVA Tet Offensive. Across the front of the searchlight cover is written the tank's callsign and the slogan "The Original Flower Children" as an ironic reminder of the era.*

RIGHT: *At the outset there was considerable opposition to the deployment of M48 medium tanks as they were thought to be heavily constrained by the terrain and the amount of technical support that they required, but in many areas of Vietnam they proved their worth on numerous operations in support of the infantry and when acting as a rapid reaction force to help beleaguered units in the field.*

OVERLEAF, LEFT: *In the field the noise of an armored unit gave the enemy plenty of warning of its approach, and in most cases the enemy withdrew rather than fight heavy AFVs. The preferred method of attack was through widespread mine warfare, often using American unexploded ordnance such as artillery shells and aerial bombs that were capable of completely destroying an M48. This one came to grief during Operation "Kentucky V" on December 20, 1967, when operating in support of B Company, 1/4th Marines.*

OVERLEAF, RIGHT: *Flying the battle flag of the Confederacy, a U.S. Army ACAV provides support to "grunts" of the 1st Marine Division during the VC/NVA Tet offensive of 1968. In Vietnam troops rarely rode inside APCs for fear of mines. By riding on top, they had more chance of survival by being blown off the vehicle if it struck a landmine, but then of course they were an easier target for the enemy if they rode outside—one of the appalling choices in wartime that might mean the difference between life and death.*

171

LEFT: *An M551 Sheridan of 3rd Squadron, 4th Cavalry Regiment, moves out on one of the first operations conducted by Sheridans in Vietnam during February 1969. Due to its light weight as an air-portable tank, the Sheridan was very vulnerable to mine attack and from RPG weapons, and this crew has fixed wire mesh to the front of the vehicle to detonate hollow-charge rounds before they strike the main armor of the tank.*

RIGHT: *Self-propelled guns were used widely in Vietnam where they were employed from fire-support bases providing the essential artillery support to infantry units operating in the field or "boonies." The M108 mounted a 105mm gun but it was soon superseded as its range and performance was inferior to the M109 155mm self-propelled howitzer based on the same chassis and turret,*

INSET, LEFT: *Nicknamed the "Duck" or simply the "V" from its designation of the V-100, the Cadillac-Gage M706 Commando was the principal armored car used by U.S. forces in Vietnam. Its main roles were for convoy escort or, in U.S. Air Force service, for the perimeter defense of air bases.*

INSET, RIGHT: *An M551 Sheridan of 3/4th Cavalry fires its 152mm main armament during gunnery training in Vietnam. Designated as an Armored Reconnaissance Airborne Assault Vehicle and not a tank, the Sheridan was rushed into combat in Vietnam before its teething problems were resolved, and it soon became unpopular with its crews—mainly due to its vulnerability to land mines, although its powerful main armament proved highly effective once its rounds were made robust enough and proof against the highly humid climatic conditions encountered in Vietnam.*

LEFT: *A graphic illustration of the difficulties of operating tanks in the hostile terrain of Vietnam. The jungle encroaches onto the road and gives excellent cover to any enemy force, while Marine engineers sweep the route for antitank mines—the scourge of AFVs in Vietnam. Standing in front of this late model M48A3 Patton is Dana Stone, one of the outstanding photographers of the war, who was killed during the invasion of Laos in 1971.*

RIGHT: *The M113 APC saw extensive service in Vietnam in many variants, of which the fifth vehicle in this line is an interesting example. This is the M113 Bridgelayer, or Marginal Terrain Assault Vehicle, that was specially developed for the Vietnam theater of operations to allow an armored unit to cross the many waterways and gullies encountered in the countryside. The first vehicle has a roll of chain link fencing across its hull front, which was erected when it stopped to provide some protection against RPG rounds.*

FAR LEFT: *The quintessential AFV of the Vietnam War was the M113 ACAV or Armored Cavalry Assault Vehicle. The ACAV was a modified M113 APC with an armored shield for the commander's M2HB Browning .50cal heavy machine gun and an additional two M60 machine guns with armored shields mounted above the troop compartment. This combination greatly increased the firepower and protection of the vehicle crew in combat.*

LEFT: *The M42A1 self-propelled anti-aircraft gun was obsolescent in its intended role of air defense in the U.S. Army but it proved highly successful in Vietnam where its twin 40mm Bofors guns proved fearsomely effective in ground support operations. This M42A1 "Duster" of 4/60th Artillery stands guard on the perimeter of a Fire Support Base in Dak To Province during Operation "Greely" in July 1967.*

LEFT: *Numerous variants of the basic M113 APC served in Vietnam such as this armored ambulance, designated as the M577A1 Field Aid Station, that provide immediate medical treatment to injured troops. This "Angel track" is operating with the 11th Armored Cavalry Regiment, the largest U.S. Army armored formation to serve in Vietnam.*

RIGHT: *Terrain remained a constant constraint to the employment of AFVs in Vietnam such as this M48A3 of Troop A of 1/1st Cavalry bogged in the mud during an operation in August 1968. This tank has a G305 turret cupola vision riser to give the crew commander better all-round vision when fighting from under armor. These devices were fitted to the final production models of the M48A3 with the designation M48A3 (Late Model).*

LEFT: *Throughout the Cold War, this is the view that every NATO tank crew dreaded—hordes of powerful T-72 MBTs sweeping across the German plains toward them in a cloud of dust and supporting artillery fire. With its low silhouette and high speed, the T-72 would have been a formidable adversary in the hands of a well-trained and motivated crew. The T-72 was exported in large numbers by the Soviet Union to over 14 countries and one of the principal customers was Iraq. They were used in large numbers during the various Gulf wars but were no match for the contemporary western tanks such as the Abrams or Challenger.*

RIGHT: *Like its T-34 predecessor, the T-54/55 series of medium tanks was produced in great numbers and was widely exported to the client states of the Soviet Union from Angola to Vietnam. It was used extensively in combat in the Middle East, during the Indo/Pakistan Wars, in Vietnam, and in Sub-Saharan Africa.*

FAR RIGHT: *Combat engineer vehicles are vital to maintain the mobility of armored forces on the offensive and equally to deny mobility to the enemy during all aspects of mechanized warfare.*

ABOVE: Throughout the 20th century, the Middle East has been the scene of many conflicts with two world wars and repeated clashes between the Israelis and the Arab nations. In 1956, the British attempted to reassert control over the Suez Canal after it had been nationalized by the Egyptian leader, Colonel Gamal Nasser. Here, a Centurion Mk. 5 of the 6th Royal Tank Regiment comes ashore at Port Said from the LST, HMS Puncher, during the initial landings on December 6, 1956.

FAR RIGHT: A graphic illustration of the horrors of mechanized warfare, as a wounded crewman struggles to extricate his injured companions from their stricken M48 Patton during the fierce fighting in the Sinai Desert. All these men are suffering from severe flash burns to their arms and faces as a medic rushes to their aid. It is a mistake to have rolled up sleeves in a tank during combat and Israeli crews were subsequently issued with flame-retardant overalls.

RIGHT: M48A2 Pattons and M3 half-tracks are prepared for battle on the eve of the Six-Day War of June 1967. At the outset of the war, the Israeli Army had 250 M48 tanks, comprising 40 M48A1 models from the Bundeswehr, 100 re-engined M48A1, and 110 M48A2Cs from U.S. sources. These vehicles equipped the 79th Battalion of the elite 7th Armored Brigade that fought a critical battle at the Rafah Junction in the opening stages of the war.

LEFT: *Prior to the Six-Day War, the Israeli Army rearmed its Centurion Mk. 5 tanks with the British-designed L7 105mm gun that proved highly successful in battle. In addition, the Centurions were fitted with a .50cal Browning M2HB machine gun at the commander's cupola.*

FAR LEFT: *Although the Centurion was most successful in battle with its heavy armor and fire-power, it was somewhat under-powered with its 650hp Meteor gasoline engine giving a top speed of just 21mph. Nevertheless, the Israelis favor heavy armor over high speed, as evinced with their first ever indigenous MBT design, the Merkava, which owes much to their experiences with the Centurion. At the time of the Six-Day War, the Israeli Army had 385 Centurions in service.*

LEFT: *The Centurion proved decisive during the fighting in the Sinai Desert in the Six-Day War, employed in both General Israel Tal's and General Abraham Yoffe's divisions in the fierce battles at Khan Yunis, Sheikh Zuweid, the Jiradi pass, Bir Larfan, the Mitla pass, and on to the Suez Canal—one of the most successful armored offensives in the annals of mechanized warfare.*

BELOW LEFT: *Peace did not come with the end of the Six-Day War and hostilities continued in a series of artillery duels and air attacks along the Suez Canal in what became known as the War of Attrition. Here, an Israeli M50 155mm self-propelled howitzer fires on Egyptian positions. The M50 was based on the chassis of the M4A3 HVSS Sherman.*

BELOW: *Following the Six-Day War, the Israeli Army modified its Centurion fleet by substituting the gasoline-powered Meteor engines with the Continental diesel AVDS-1790 powerplant that was the same as that in the M48 and M60 tanks. The upgraded version of the Centurion was known as Shot (whip) and is easily identified by the modified rear hull to accommodate the larger engine.*

INSET: *A Centurion Shot kicks up the dust as it grinds across the desert towards the Suez Canal. The modifications to the basic Centurion undertaken by the Israeli Army produced a tank with the three fundamental design aspects of firepower, armor protection, and mobility matched to fine degree with the equally important factor of survivability in battle. The Shot was known for its ability to suffer battle damage but keep on fighting, which made it popular with its crews.*

BELOW: *A column of M60A1 Pattons advances across the Sinai Desert towards the Suez Canal during the Israeli counteroffensive in the October War of 1973. The Israeli Army procured 150 M60A1 Pattons prior to the October War and they served exclusively on the Sinai Front. In Israeli service, both the M48 and M60 are known as Magach and a much modified form, the M60 Magach, continues to serve with the Israeli Army to this day.*

INSET: *The venerable M4 Sherman continued in Israeli service during the October War but in a much modified form—known as the M51HV or Isherman, for Israeli Sherman. This model featured a French VO980 105mm smooth-bore gun and a Cummins VT8-460 460hp diesel engine. Here, an M51HV tows a disabled companion tank past a knocked-out T-55 during the fighting on the Golan Heights on October 9, 1973.*

BELOW: *A formation of mixed Shot and Centurion tanks advances across the barren Golan Heights during the Israeli counterattack after the initial savage battles of the Syrian armored onslaught that almost reached the Jordan River. The Centurion on the left is an original gasoline powered model while that on the right is an upgraded Shot.*

FAR LEFT: *One of the bitter lessons of the October War was the massive consumption of ammunition, which was way beyond all estimates. Within days Israel was running perilously low on tank rounds and thousands were airlifted from U.S. bases in America and Europe to allow the IDF to continue fighting. Postwar statistics reveal that it took 40 rounds of tank ammunition to destroy one enemy AFV.*

LEFT: *The Israeli offensive in the Sinai Desert was a masterly counterstroke that allowed the IDF to cross the Suez Canal and surround the Egyptian Third Army—a move that precipitated a ceasefire on October 23, 1973. Here, mechanized infantry in their elderly M3 half-tracks cross the Suez and Sweetwater Canals under the covering guns of a disabled Shot in the final days of the war.*

ABOVE: *The modern concept of mechanized warfare demands the close integration of combined-arms teams comprising armor, infantry, artillery, and airpower for maximum flexibility and effect on the battlefield.*

RIGHT: *2,705 M24 Chaffee light tanks were supplied to NATO nations after World War II and they remained in service for many years. In 1972, the Norwegian Army upgraded 54 Chaffees, incorporating a NAPCO 6V53T diesel engine derived from that of the M113 APC coupled to an Allison MT-653 transmission, and mounting a French D-925 90mm low pressure gun in place of the original 75mm. A new fire control system was also fitted with a Simrad LV3 laser rangefinder above the barrel. The tank was designated NM-116 and featured a colorful splinter camouflage scheme.*

OPPOSITE, ABOVE: *Named after General Omar Bradley of World War II fame, the M2 Bradley was the first truly mechanized infantry fighting vehicle or IFV of the U.S. Army. The first Bradleys were delivered in May 1981 and two years later they were issued to units of the 3rd Infantry Division (Mechanized) in Europe.*

OPPOSITE, BELOW: *The primary purpose of any tank is to dominate the battlefield with accurate fire from its large-caliber main armament. To this end tank gunnery is a vital skill that must be practiced repeatedly. NATO nations were always outnumbered in tanks by the Warsaw Pact, so the only way to overcome this disparity was through superior weapons systems and better crew training.*

RIGHT AND INSETS: *During the Cold War, NATO tanks were generally better equipped for night fighting than those of the Warsaw Pact. Originally infra-red (IR) headlights and search-lights were fitted to allow movement and combat at night, but IR has the disadvantage of being readily detectable by an enemy with similar equipment. Accordingly, when the Warsaw Pact saw the widespread introduction of IR, NATO introduced passive night observation devices and, latterly, thermal imaging to maintain their superiority over Soviet tank designs until the end of the Cold War.*

OPPOSITE: *With the Lion Rampant flag flying high, a Chieftain Mk. 5/3C of the 4th Troop, CAT Squadron, of The Royal Scots Dragoon Guards moves off on a battle run during the Canadian Army Trophy NATO tank gunnery competition at Bergen-Hohne in West Germany, June 1983.*

LEFT: *A pair of Leopard 1A3 tanks acts as a roadblock during Exercise "Certain Challenge" in West Germany. For decades, NATO mounted massive field exercises to test its preparedness for war with the Warsaw Pact, causing much disruption for the local populace and farmers as their land was churned up by hundreds of tanks and AFVs—but such was the price of deterrence and peace in Europe.*

BELOW: *Throughout the Cold War there were many attempts to develop joint tank projects between NATO partners, as a successful venture would reduce procurement costs and increase "interoperability" within the various armies. The Warsaw Pact had a great advantage as all member states were obliged to use Soviet designs, be it the T-54/55 series, T-62, or T-72. In the late 1960s, West Germany and the United States developed the MBT-70 but it proved to be too complex and expensive and was cancelled after the expenditure of vast amounts of money. The Germans went on to design and produce the Leopard 2, which has proved to be a most successful design. The Leopard 2 has been adopted by several NATO and European neutral countries and by default has become the "Standard NATO" MBT.*

OPPOSITE, LEFT: *The tank commander of an M60 Patton pumps out rounds from his M85 cupola-mounted M2HB Browning .50cal heavy machine gun during target practice. The M85 commander's cupola was a feature of the M60 series but it was overly complex and raised the tank's height to an unacceptable degree. In Israeli service the cupola was removed and replaced by a simple hatch.*

OPPOSITE, RIGHT: *Like all Soviet tanks, the T-72 was produced in large numbers with the best models being reserved for the Red Army and its chosen Warsaw Pact partners while simpler versions were exported to other countries.*

ABOVE AND RIGHT: *One of the principal lessons of World War II was the necessity to provide the infantry with a fully enclosed APC for movement on the battlefield rather than the open-topped half-tracks and tank hulls used in the war. Both wheeled and tracked APCs appeared in the 1950s, with the most important US type being the M113 series (top left). The M113 has been highly successful and it was produced in greater numbers than any other AFV. Being lightly armored and armed with a single heavy machine gun, the M113 acted as a "battlefield taxi" to deliver troops to the battle zone where they fought dismounted. With the emergence of the nuclear battlefield, the need arose for the infantry to have greater protection and the capacity to engage and destroy other AFVs, particularly other APCs. The result was the infantry fighting vehicle of today— such as the M2 Bradley illustrated here with its two-man turret armed with a 25mm Bushmaster cannon capable of destroying other IFVs and light armor, while on the side of the turret is TOW missile launcher for engaging MBTs out to a distance of 4,000yd.*

OPPOSITE: *Painted in the multi-color MERDC camouflage scheme, M113A1 APCs and M60A1 tanks of the 1/67th Armor Regiment, 2nd Armored Division, are loaded aboard Heavy Equipment Transports (HET) at Fort Hood in 1981. The HET or tank transporter is a vital component of mechanized warfare to carry MBTs and other AFVs over long distances to save expensive wear and tear on their tracks and automotive systems. The average life span of a set of tank tracks can be in the order of 850 miles.*

ABOVE: *A Leopard 1A1 of the 1st Lancers takes part in the NATO field exercise "Certain Strike 87." The Belgian Army procured a total of 334 Leopard 1 MBTs and they formed the main striking force of 1st (Belgian) Corps stationed in West Germany as part of NORTHAG. In time of war, the two divisions of 1st (BE) Corps were responsible for a frontage of 62 miles between Kassel and Aachen.*

RIGHT: *The Centurion was a most successful tank design and many were supplied to NATO countries by America under the Mutual Defense Armament Program during the 1950s. Flying the national flag of Denmark, this modernized Centurion Mk. 5 of the Guard Hussar Regiment, Seeland Division, awaits orders to advance during Exercise "Eternal Triangle" in 1986.*

LEFT: The M1 Abrams series is the current Main Battle Tank (MBT) of the U.S. Army. It was developed after the demise of the American/German joint MBT-70 project. Two competing prototype models were designed by Chrysler (now General Dynamics Land Systems) and General Motors with the former being chosen for full-scale production. The first model, the M1, was armed with the s tandard 105mm gun. It appeared in 1980 with an improved version with additional armor protection in 1984—an example of which is shown here with the 1st Cavalry Division on the West German plains during Exercise "Certain Strike 87."

ABOVE: Since World War II, U.S. tank design has been evolutionary rather than revolutionary until the advent of the M1 Abrams. The M60 series can trace its lineage back through the years to the M46, which was the first tank to bear the famous name Patton. The M60A3 shown here was the last in line of over 15,000 M60 MBTs built between 1960 and 1987. The M60 has served in 20 countries beside the U.S. Army and U.S. Marine Corps, and remains a potent MBT to this day. Armed with the M68A1 (a version of the British L7) 105mm gun, the M60A3 features a computerized fire-control system with a laser rangefinder and thermal imaging night vision devices. It carries 63 rounds of main armament ammunition with 900 for the commander's heavy machine gun and 5,950 rounds for the coaxial 7.62mm machine gun. With its reliable Continental 750hp 12-cylinder diesel engine, the M60A3 is capable of 30mph to a range of 300 miles.

LEFT AND RIGHT: *A Leopard 2A4 of the 2nd Company, 33 Panzerbattalion, lies waiting in an ambush position in the treeline, its turret well camouflaged with netting as the loader mans the external MG3 7.62mm machine gun. The Bundeswehr—the then West German army—procured a total of 2,125 Leopard 2 MBTs to equip their armored brigades. At the height of the Cold War, the West German army deployed 17 Panzer brigades and 15 Panzergrenadier or mechanized brigades. Whereas the Leopard 2 was the main MBT of the Panzer brigades, the Leopard 1 provided the MBT strength within the Panzergrenadier brigades. The West German army had a total of 2,437 Leopard 1 MBTs with the Panzerwaffe forming the most powerful armored force within NATO facing the Iron Curtain that was the Inner German Border until 1989.*

RIGHT: *The Leopard 2 series is arguably the most successful of the current generation of MBTs and it is in service with the armies of Austria, Denmark, Germany, Greece, Netherlands, Poland, Spain, Sweden, and Switzerland. Like all great tank designs, it combines the attributes of firepower, armor and mobility to a high degree. It is armed with a smooth-bore 120mm Rheinmetall gun; it is protected by the latest laminated combination armor and is powered by 1,500hp MTU MB 873 Ka 501 12-cylinder diesel engine that gives an excellent power to weight ratio of 27hp per ton and a top speed of 44mph as well as outstanding cross-country agility. It has been progressively upgraded and the latest models incorporate even better armor protection and firepower with an extended L/55 gun. It carries 42 rounds of 120mm ammunition but its sophisticated fire-control system ensures that every round counts in any tank engagement.*

FAR RIGHT: *Following World War II experience, the tank producing nations drew different conclusions: the Germans were convinced that heavy tanks such as the Tiger I and II were too unwieldy to be truly successful; the British and the Americans, on the other hand, had fought the war with tanks that were consistently undergunned and poorly armored albeit with greater tactical and strategic mobility. The Americans and British went on to develop much heavier tanks such as the M60 and the Chieftain, whereas the Germans preferred the much lighter Leopard 1. The French followed the German school of thought and after a failed joint venture between the two countries, France produced the AMX30 weighing just 79,000lb as against 121,000lb for Chieftain or 107,500lb for the M60. These AMX30 MBTs of the 507th RCC (Régiment des Chars de Combat) are shown during a maintenance halt in a village in Champagne during a field exercise with the 12th Light Armored Division.*

After World War II, the British Army resolved never to go into battle again with a tank that was inferior in firepower or armor protection to any enemy. After the success of the L7 105mm tank gun that became virtually universal among NATO nations, the British introduced the 120mm main armament on the Chieftain and its successor Challenger, shown here negotiating a knife-edge obstacle displaying the great length of its powerful 120mm L11A5 gun. The Challenger was the first production tank to feature Chobham armor that has revolutionized the protection of tanks and AFVs.

FAR LEFT: *Although a potent and powerful MBT, the Challenger relied on a similar fire-control system to that of Chieftain. This was not so capable as those of contemporary MBTs such as the M1 Abrams or Leopard 2, but the TOGS thermal-imaging night-vision equipment was outstanding for the time. Firing from prepared fire positions such as that shown here, Challenger was a formidable opponent with the emphasis on long-range accurate fire from the halt, with great survivability to obtain the required kill ratio against Warsaw Pact tanks of 10 to 1.*

LEFT: *In spite of its unhappy service during the Vietnam War, the M551 Sheridan continued as a reconnaissance tank in armored formations and as the air-portable fire-support vehicle in airborne divisions for rapid deployment to trouble spots around the world. It was in this guise that the Sheridan was the first U.S. AFV to arrive in Saudi Arabia at the outset of Operation "Desert Shield" after the Iraqi invasion of Kuwait in 1990.*

OVERLEAF: *Leopard 2A4 MBTs of Pantserbataljon 43, 41st Armored Brigade, 4th Division of the Royal Netherlands Army, act as "enemy" for the 1st Cavalry Division during "Reforger 87" —the annual major U.S. exercise to test the Return of Forces to Germany strategy of reinforcing Europe with units from the U.S. in times of tension. The Leopard 2 has proved to be very successful in Dutch service and 180 MBTs have been upgraded to 2A5 standard with the new Rheinmetall 120mm 55 caliber gun and an improved range of ammunition as well as a battlefield management system and enhanced turret armor protection.*

RIGHT: *The Spanish armed forces were long-term users of the M48 Patton; 18 were in service with the Spanish Marine Corps as tank support during amphibious landings to supplement the Scorpion CVR(T) vehicles that provided support during initial landings with LVTP7 Amtracs. Original M48 models were armed with the standard 90mm main armament but these were upgraded to the M48A5E2 standard in Spain—164 saw service. Those in the Spanish Marines were superseded by 16 of the M60A3E model—the E standing for Espana to indicate the various modifications added in Spain.*

FAR RIGHT: *The Scorpion CVR(T) range has been exported worldwide with over 3,000 vehicles in service with 20 armies from Botswana to Venezuela. This Scorpion is used by the Spanish Marines as fire support for their LVTP7 amphibious assault vehicles during seaborne landings. The Spanish Marines are equipped with 17 LVTPA1 Amtracs and 17 diesel-powered Scorpions.*

LEFT: *The basic component of any army is the foot soldier, as he or she remains the only means to occupy ground on the battlefield. The whole panoply of weapon systems serves the infantryman to achieve this end. In many ways, warfare is as simple as that.*

BELOW: *The cost of a modern MBT is extremely high, so many armies prefer to procure modernized older tanks or have them as a secondary part of the overall tank fleet. A typical example is the M48 Patton that remains in service across the world in various guises. The original 90mm gun of the M48 has been replaced by the M68/L7 105mm and most feature a modern diesel engine, a new fire-control system, and night vision equipment. In addition, the overly large commander's machine gun cupola is usually replaced by a simple hatch. In the mid-1970s, the U.S. Army upgraded many earlier M48 models to this new standard—designated M48A5. These were subsequently exported widely and the M48A5 has seen service with the armies of Greece, Jordan, South Korea, Lebanon, Morocco, Pakistan, Portugal, Spain, Taiwan, Thailand, Tunisia, and Turkey. Other countries such as West Germany and Israel have devised their own upgrade programs for outdated M48s.*

ABOVE: *Introduced in 1966, the AMX30 incorporated a 105mm smooth-bore gun firing fin-stabilized ammunition that allows a heavier weapon to be mounted in a lighter vehicle than in conventional designs. Thanks to aggressive French marketing techniques, the AMX30 has seen service with the armies of Bosnia, Chile, Croatia, France, Qatar, Saudi Arabia, Spain, United Arab Emirates, and Venezuela. This AMX30 is being decontaminated with high pressure hoses in a simulated NBC exercise.*

LEFT: *Between 1965 and 1970, 1,700 M551 Sheridans were produced by General Motors. The most notable feature of the Sheridan was its M81 152mm gun/missile launcher. The weapon fired a variety of rounds including the wire-guided Shillelagh missile in the anti-armor role. The Sheridan was over complex and required to undertake too many roles that in the end it was incapable of fulfilling any of them adequately and it was withdrawn from front-line service from the late 1970s. Since then the chassis has been modified to resemble Soviet or Russian AFVs that act as OPFOR (Opposing Forces) at the National Training Center.*

After many years of using wheeled armored cars for reconnaissance duties, the British Army turned to tracked vehicles in 1969 with the introduction of a family of AFVs designated Combat Vehicle Reconnaissance (Tracked) or CVR(T). This comprised numerous different models: Scorpion, armed with a 76mm gun for fire support; Striker, armed with Swingfire anti-tank guided missiles; the Spartan APC; Stormer, a larger APC or command vehicle; the Sultan command vehicle; the Samaritan armored ambulance; the Samson recovery vehicle; and, shown here, the Scimitar reconnaissance vehicle armed with a potent 30mm cannon capable of destroying most contemporary light AFVs on the battlefield. A further reconnaissance vehicle to Scimitar in service with the British Army is Sabre, which combines the hull of a Scorpion and the turret of a Fox armoured car. With their low weight and high mobility, the Scorpion, Scimitar, and Samson CVR(T) models proved particularly effective across the boggy and hostile terrain encountered during the Falklands War in 1982.

Designed soon after World War II, the AMX13 is a most innovative vehicle as its main armament, originally a 75mm derived from that of the Panther and subsequently a 90mm, is mounted in an oscillating turret whereby the upper part with the fixed gun pivots around the lower section. This allows an automatic loader to be incorporated, with the 12 rounds in rotating magazines in the rear bustle of the turret. This reduces the crew to three men and makes the vehicle more compact, but such a small number of rounds before reloading becomes necessary is a tactical disadvantage. The AMX13 has sold in large numbers around the world and it remains in widespread service together with a family of variants.

ABOVE: *Designed by Degtyarev and Shpagin, which gave rise to the designation of DShK 1938 12.7mm or .50cal heavy machine gun, the "Dushka" has been the standard antiaircraft weapon on Soviet tanks since World War II.*

RIGHT: *Soviet tank designs have always emphasized the basic essentials of firepower, mobility, and armor protection as epitomised by the T-54/55 series. Although cramped and crude by western standards, it suited the temperament and mentality of the Soviet soldier and the Soviet style of warfare as well as being produced in greater numbers than any other tank.*

LEFT: *The M1 Abrams was the first production tank to feature a gas turbine engine as part of its powerplant. The advantages of the gas turbine are that it is more compact for a given power output and it is simple to maintain. The Textron Lycoming AGT-1500 turbine linked to an Allison X1100-3B hydrokinetic transmission also gives high acceleration for a tank weighing over 60 tons and gives a top speed of 42mph. Other radical features of the M1 include a separated compart-ment divorced from the crew for the stowage of the main armament ammunition. This has blow-out panels in its roof so if the turret is hit and the ammunition explodes, the blast is vented upward and away from the crew compartment. The markings on the side of this M1 Abrams indicates it belongs to the 3rd Platoon of A Company within the tank battalion.*

RIGHT: *The T-72 was exported in large numbers by the Soviet Union to over 14 countries and one of the principal customers was Iraq. They were used in large numbers during the various Gulf wars but were no match for the contemporary western tanks such as the Abrams or Challenger.*

BELOW: *The T-72M was the principal MBT of the Iraqi Republican Guard formations. Although they fought tenaciously at times, they were hopelessly outclassed technically and tactically by the Coalition Forces. Although the 125mm main armament of the T-72 is on a par with the 120mm types of the M1 Abrams and Challenger 1, it was consistently outfought as most engagements took place at night or in foul weather when the thermal-imaging equipment of the western tanks proved far superior: the T-72s were destroyed before they even realized the Coalition forces were in the vicinity. Not a single Abrams or Challenger was disabled by a T-72 during the 100 hours of the land campaign.*

INSET: *Tanks and jet planes remain the favorite toys of dictators of all persuasions, and they are bought in vast quantities, mainly from the former Soviet Union. The cost to the poor unfortunate countries they tyrannize is incalculable, as most of these weapon systems end up as scrap metal littering the deserts of the Middle East from Nasser's vaulted ambitions in the Sinai to Saddam's cataclysmic failures in Iran and Kuwait.*

TOP: *AFVs of the 2nd Armored Cavalry Regiment congregate on the desert sands of the intermediate staging area near the disembarkation port of Jubail in Saudi Arabia during the build-up of Operation "Desert Shield." The 2nd Armored Cavalry Regiment was involved in one of the most decisive engagements of the war known as the "Battle for 73 Easting" against the 50th Brigade of the Iraqi 12th Armored Division during which, in one 23-minute encounter, Eagle Troop destroyed 28 Iraqi tanks and about 50 other AFVs.*

ABOVE: *As part of the Coalition Forces against Saddam Hussein, the British Army deployed the 1st UK Armoured Division to Saudi Arabia in support of Operation "Desert Shield." This photograph shows several of the different types of AFVs deployed by the British on Operation "Granby." In the back row, from left to right, are a Ferret armored car, a Sultan CVR(T) command vehicle, and Challenger 1 MBTs. In the foreground is the FV432 APC (the British equivalent of the M113) and beside it the Warrior IFV (the British equivalent of the Bradley). This photograph was taken soon after deployment into the desert as the Warriors have not as yet been uparmored with Chobam armor panels along their sides.*

BELOW: *Strapped to the back of a transporter of a Saudi trucking company, an M1A1 of 3rd Battalion, 32nd Armored Regiment, is moved westwards to the forming-up positions for Operation "Desert Saber." 3/32 Armor was part of the 1st Cavalry Division within the U.S. Army's VIIth Corps. A tank battalion comprised 55 tanks with 14 M1A1 MBTs in each of four companies and two in the headquarters company. The downward pointing chevron denotes that this tank belonged to C Company. Although simpler and more reliable than diesels, the gas turbine engine of the M1 Abrams consumes fuel at a gargantuan rate requiring far more fuel bowsers in support but any perceived advantage in a tank design comes at a price.*

LEFT: *The U.S. Marine Corps committed considerable assets to Operation "Desert Shield" and then Operation "Desert Saber." The principal USMC AFVs were the M60 and M1 MBTs and the LVTP7A1 or Landing Vehicle Tracked Personnel Model 7. The LVTP7 or Amtrac is fully amphibious, reflecting the Marine Corps' role as the U.S. Navy's assault force from the sea. On land it also acts as an APC, albeit a somewhat bulky one due to its boat-like configuration. Capable of carrying 25 troops and a crew of three, the Amtrac is armed with a .50cal heavy machine gun and a 40mm grenade launcher in a turret designated the Upgunned Weapons Station.*

BELOW: *M113 APCs of the Arab Joint Force Command drive cautiously down the newly recaptured streets of Kuwait City following the withdrawal of Iraqi troops in February 1991. As the Coalition Forces closed in on the Kuwaiti capital, it was left to the Kuwaiti 35th Armored Brigade and Task Force Muthana to liberate the city itself.*

RIGHT AND FAR RIGHT: *A BMP-1 lies abandoned in the desert. After weeks of incessant bombardment from the air, most Iraqi soldiers were only too keen to abandon their equipment and Saddam's cause at the earliest opportunity. In any disciplined army, equipment is always destroyed to forego its capture and use by the enemy, but many Iraqi vehicles were fully serviceable. With its fuel cells in the rear doors, the BMP-1 was particularly susceptible to fire when hit and it was no match for the M2 Bradley seen storming across the desert (far right). It is estimated that the Iraqi army lost as many as 3,700 AFVs during the Gulf War of 1990–91.*

The awesome combat power of a modern armored formation is shown to full effect in this photograph of the Challenger 1 MBTs of D Squadron, 14th/20th Royal Hussars, standing ready at the head of the Royal Regiment of Fusiliers Battlegroup of the 4th Armoured Brigade, 1st UK Armoured Division, as it prepares for Operation "Desert Saber." Attached to the U.S. Army's VIIth Corps, the 1st UK Armoured Division was part of the major offensive to liberate Kuwait in February 1991.

BELOW: *Warrior Infantry Fighting Vehicles of the 1st Battalion, The Cheshire Regiment, pause during an UNPROFOR (United Nations Protection Force) operation in Bosnia in early 1993. The Warriors are fitted with Chobham armor panels along the hull sides to defeat attack from RPG weapons. The vehicle in the foreground is an FV512 Mechanised Combat Vehicle (Repair) towing a 6.5-tonne High Mobility Maintenance Support Trailer carrying spare parts for the Warriors.*

RIGHT: *A Bison armored personnel carrier moves out of the base camp of the 2nd Battalion, The Royal Canadian Regiment during a patrol in Bosnia in 1996 as part of IFOR (Implementation Force) in the former Republic Yugoslavia. The Bison is manufactured by the Diesel Division, General Motors of Canada and 149 were procured by the Canadian army with a further 50 specialised variants such as command vehicles and mortar carriers.*

LEFT: *A tank commander of an M1A1 Abrams of 1st Cavalry Division engages Iraqi insurgents in Fallujah in April 2004 with his .50cal machine gun. While the M1 Abrams is one of the most modern AFVs in the U.S. Army, the M2HB Browning heavy machine gun is one of the oldest weapons in its inventory. First introduced in 1925, the M2 Browning was progressively improved until World War II when 1,968,596 were produced.*

FAR LEFT: *A U.S. Marine Corps Light Armored Vehicle 25 patrols through the streets of Fallujah in May 2004. Built by the Diesel Division, General Motors of Canada, the LAV 25 was first procured by the U.S. Marine Corps in October 1983 as a highly mobile amphibious IFV with a crew of three and six troops in the rear compartment. It is armed with a 25mm Bushmaster cannon and two 7.62mm machine guns. There are numerous variants of the basic vehicle and the LAV is also employed by the Canadian army as the Bison and by the U.S. Army as the Stryker.*

LEFT: *Troops of Charlie Company, 2nd Battalion, 3rd Infantry Division from the 3rd Brigade of the 2nd Infantry Division Stryker Brigade Combat Team secure a helicopter landing zone outside the city of Mosul on Independence Day, 2004, as members of the Iraq Survey Group fly in to test for possible weapons of mass destruction.*

An M2A3 Bradley of Bravo Company, 1st Battalion, 116th Infantry Regiment, 1st Infantry Division—the "Big Red One"—provides cover as troops search a former Iraqi army base at Ramadi for weapons and munitions on February 8, 2004.

RIGHT: The crew of an M2A3 Bradley IFV keep a wary watch as engineers sweep the road for IEDs (Improvised Explosive Devices) which pose the most serious threat to AFVs in Iraq. Note the TOW missile launcher on the left-hand side of the turret that allows the Bradley to engage targets out to a range of 4,000yd.

LEFT: *Soldiers of the "Renegade" Platoon, Bravo Company, 2/8th Infantry Regiment, conduct a raid in a village in the Diyala Province during Operation "Iraqi Freedom" on August 28, 2003, with their M3A3 Bradley IFV in the background.*

RIGHT: *Even in the most mechanized armies in the world, it still comes down to boots on the ground in the end —or, in this case, in the swamp as Marines from C Company, 1st Engineers of BCT-1 conduct a Security and Stabilization Operation in the Al Anbar Province of Iraq on June 10, 2004, under the covering fire of an M113A3 APC.*

BELOW: *An M3A3 Bradley of Eagle Troop, 2nd Squadron, 3rd Armored Cavalry Regiment, kicks up the dust as it storms across the desert northeast of Fallujah during Operation "Iraqi Freedom."*

ABOVE: *An M1A1 Abrams MBT of A Company, 1st Battalion, 35th Armor Regiment from the 1st Armored Division patrols through the streets of Baghdad on November 13, 2003.*

FAR RIGHT: *Soldiers of Comanche Company, 1st Battalion, 23rd Infantry Regiment of the 2nd Infantry Division dismount from their Stryker Infantry Carrier Vehicle to conduct a search operation in Mosul on May 13, 2004. These troops are part of the Stryker Brigade Combat Team and are equipped with the highly effective Stryker family of AFVs.*

RIGHT: *Accepted doctrine dictates that heavy MBTs are ill-suited to urban combat, but the M1 Abrams proved to be brutally effective during the reoccupation of Fallujah during Operation "Phantom Fury" in November 2004. As a vital component in the combined arms team of infantry, artillery, and airpower, armor remains the potent force that dominates the battlefield with its direct fire weapons.*

FAR RIGHT: *An M2A3 Bradley IFV patrols the Abu Ghurayb Market area of Baghdad in November 2003 during Operation "Iraqi Freedom." The turret is traversed to the rear with the commander manning a roof-mounted 7.62mm machine gun for close-in defense.*

The distinctive "Big Red One" shoulder patch indicates soldiers of the 1st Infantry Division as they conduct a routine patrol with their M998 Hummers—High Mobility Multi-Purpose Wheeled Vehicle—on January 16, 2004, near Ar Ramadia in Iraq. By the year 2000, over 140,000 Hummers had been built with the U.S. Armed Forces procuring many of the armored version—known as the M1114—for service in high-threat areas such as Bosnia and Iraq.

LEFT: The M109 155mm self-propelled howitzer has been in service with the U.S. Army since the Vietnam War but it remains a highly effective weapon system to this day. These M109A6 howitzers of Charlie Battery, 4th Battalion, 1st Field Artillery are conducting a live firing exercise outside Baghdad on December 11, 2003.

LEFT: *A pair of M1A1 Abrams MBTs of 2nd Battalion, 63rd Armor Regiment of the 1st Infantry Division return from a firefight with insurgent forces in Ba'qubah on June 24, 2004.*

ABOVE: *Seen thru an image intensifier, a Bradley IFV of the 1st Squadron, 9th Cavalry of the 1st Cavalry Division, provides covering fire during a large-scale search operation in the Talaa Square area of Baghdad on July 22, 2004. U.S. troops and AFVs have excellent night vision devices that give them a significant tactical advantage during the hours of darkness that allows them to conduct operations on a 24-hour basis as required.*

TOP: *An M9 Combat Earth Mover clears on obstruction from a road in Baghdad that is suspected of hiding an IED. Specialized combat engineer equipment is a vital component of the combined arms team to clear obstacles, mines and a host of other threats on the battlefield.*

A superb study of a Bradley IFV in its latest guise as the M2A3 with the full array of both passive and active supplementary armor panels on the hull front and sides and a commander's independent viewer on the turret roof to the left of his position as seen. These Bradleys and HUMVEE of the 39th Brigade Combat Team are on patrol near the town of Al Taji on August 1, 2004.